D'OYLY CARTE'S OPERA COMPANY.

YZANCE

ARTHUR SULLIVAN.

D'OYLY CARTE.

S. GILBERT.

J.C. BAKER

CH	DE ✓
KH	MF ✓
RA	

GILBERT & SULLIVAN
THE D'OYLY CARTE YEARS

GILBERT & SULLIVAN
THE D'OYLY CARTE YEARS

Robin Wilson

Frederic Lloyd

Weidenfeld and Nicolson London

ENDPAPERS **An American poster for** *The Pirates of Penzance*, **1880.**

PAGE 1 **Dudley Hardy's poster for** *The Yeomen of the Guard*, **1897.**

PAGE 2 **John Hassall's poster for** *The Gondoliers*, **1919.**

PAGE 3 **H. M. Brock's poster for** *Princess Ida*, **1919.**

PAGES 4–5 **H. M. Brock's posters for** *Iolanthe* **and** *Patience*, **1919.**

Contents

Forewords by *Dame Bridget D'Oyly Carte, D.B.E.* and *John Reed, O.B.E.*	*6*
Introduction by *Lord Wilson of Rievaulx*	*7*
Preface	*8*
The D'Oyly Carte Family	*9*
The Curtain Rises	*10*
Early Days	*50*
The Henry Lytton Years	*88*
The Martyn Green Years	*126*
The Peter Pratt Years	*152*
The John Reed Years	*176*
The Curtain Falls	*206*
Bibliography	*214*
Index of Operas and Plays	*214*
Index of Names	*214*
Acknowledgements	*216*

First published in Great Britain by George Weidenfeld & Nicolson Limited 91 Clapham High Street, London SW4 7TA

ISBN 0 297 78505 2

Designed by Rick Fawcett/Dark Design
Edited by Linda A. Doeser

Printed by BAS Printers Limited, Over Wallop, Hampshire
Colour separations by Newsele Litho Limited, Italy

Foreword
Dame Bridget D'Oyly Carte

Robin Wilson and Frederic Lloyd have collected a great many illustrations for this book, from the U.S.A. and England, that will, I am sure, be of interest to Gilbert and Sullivan enthusiasts in both countries.

It gives a splendid indication of the developments that have taken place over the years and the way in which changes in fashion, both in production and visual approach, have evolved quite naturally through the work of the various producers and designers who have been associated with the Gilbert and Sullivan operas at different periods.

The authors' knowledge, hard work and enthusiasm deserve support, and the book has all my good wishes.

Bridget D'Oyly Carte

Foreword
John Reed, O.B.E.

With the greatest of pleasure I write this Foreword for your book on the history of the D'Oyly Carte Company over the last 100 years. Out of those 100 years I did 28 – 28 years of wonderful experiences, very good friendships, exciting travel and, of course, Gilbert and Sullivan. I joined as a novice – in point of fact I told Mr Frederic Lloyd so at my audition, to which he replied 'Good, we can start you off the way we mean you to carry on.' I sincerely hope that I 'carried on' in the true tradition of the Company.

Those years were the happiest of my career on the stage. My reward has always been the warmth and affection shown to me by the appreciative audiences in theatres throughout the world.

It only remains for me to say, 'Thank you most sincerely' to Dame Bridget and all associated with this book.

John Reed

TOP LEFT **Arthur Sullivan (Kenneth Sandford) and W. S. Gilbert (Donald Adams) help Bridget D'Oyly Carte cut a cake to celebrate the 75th anniversary of** *The Mikado.*

TOP RIGHT **John Reed, wearing the O.B.E. medal awarded him in 1977, holds up the record issued to commemorate his first 25 years with the Company.**

RIGHT **Lord Wilson (then Sir Harold) with the Company outside the House of Lords.**

Introduction
Lord Wilson of Rievaulx

I have been asked by the Publishers of this D'Oyly Carte book to write a brief note on our family's connections with the Gilbert and Sullivan operas and with the D'Oyly Carte Company.

Each year our chapel choir in the Colne Valley, near Huddersfield, attempted one of the G & S operas until, baulking at what we felt to be an extortionate royalty demand of two guineas, we disloyally presented the alien production *Floradora*. There were threats of the valley running with blood at our apostasy and soon we were back with the Masters. When we staged *H.M.S. Pinafore* I was, at the age of ten, technically a principal – the result of W. S. Gilbert's quirkish decision to include the non-speaking, non-singing Midshipmite, Tom Tucker, in that enviable list. All I can remember from that production is being sent off the stage in disgrace during a performance for sucking a bulls-eye given to me by Little Buttercup.

A few years later, having moved by this time to Merseyside, I saw my first D'Oyly Carte performance. In October 1933 I was taken by one of our schoolmasters to the Liverpool Empire to see Sir Henry Lytton in *The Yeomen of the Guard*. It was at a later performance of the same opera, in March 1956, that my son Robin, one of the compilers of this book, fell in love with the Gilbert and Sullivan operas.

My own involvement with the D'Oyly Carte Opera Company began during my last premiership, when I was talk-ing to Sir Hugh Wontner, the Lord Mayor of London. Sir Hugh asked me if I was interested in the D'Oyly Carte Company and invited me to the Centenary Performance of *Trial by Jury* on March 25, 1975. I made a short speech from the stage at the end of that Centenary night and soon afterwards I accepted Dame Bridget's invitation to become a Trustee. I still treasure those meetings at the Savoy.

In 1976, on reaching 60, I resigned the premiership. To my farewell party I invited Dame Bridget D'Oyly Carte, Frederic Lloyd and other leading D'Oyly Carte figures – management and principals. At one point I passed around slips of paper for each to note down their three favourite G & S operas and was pleased to find that Dame Bridget and I had chosen the same three operas – *Iolanthe, Pirates* and *Yeomen*.

The following year I had the pleasure of attending a performance of *H.M.S. Pinafore* which the Company had the enviable honour of presenting before H.M. The Queen at Windsor Castle. This was a very memorable occasion and stands out among the performances of the Company that I attended in its final years.

In the penultimate season I joined the Company on the top of an open bus in a tour of Westminster. The men in the Company were wearing their Peers' costumes from *Iolanthe*, and the occasion was designed to attract attention to the Company's plight. But it was all to no avail – on February 27, 1982, the D'Oyly Carte closed its doors. Since then, former members of the cast have kept the memory fresh by training new generations of amateur performers, while our 'Friends of D'Oyly Carte' keep the name and the memories alive.

Let me end by welcoming this book on the Company and by putting on record that my knowledge of D'Oyly Carte does not constitute one small fraction of the expertise of the compilers of this authoritative volume.

Preface

On February 27, 1982 the curtain came down for the last time on a performance by the D'Oyly Carte Opera Company. This Company was formed in the 1870s by the impresario Richard D'Oyly Carte for the express purpose of performing the operas of W. S. Gilbert and Arthur Sullivan. After presenting these operas almost continuously for 107 years, the Company was forced to close through lack of financial support.

The final performance took place on the last night of the 1981–82 season at the Adelphi Theatre, London. It was played to a capacity audience, some of whom had queued for days to get seats. As was customary at the last night of a London season, the Company endeavoured to make the occasion a joyous and humorous one. But in spite of the jollifications, there was a great feeling of sadness as the audience saw their favourite performers for the last time.

It was on this historic occasion that we formulated the idea of compiling a pictorial history of the D'Oyly Carte Company. There is a wealth of visual material, ranging from photographs and drawings to posters, programmes, stage sets and costume designs. Much of this material has not previously appeared in book form.

We have been extremely fortunate in the amount of help that we have received. When we mentioned this project to Dame Bridget D'Oyly Carte, she very kindly gave us access to all the material in the D'Oyly Carte archives. In addition, she agreed to write a Foreword and has been unstinting with her time and advice during the past two years. We are very grateful to John Reed for contributing a Foreword and to Lord Wilson for his Introduction. The authors and publisher would also like to thank Lord Hanson for the generous help which made this book possible.

Much of the early archive material in this book is located in the Theatre Museum and we very much appreciate the help given to us by Catherine Haill and her colleagues. A few items come from the Reginald Allen Collection at the Pierpont Morgan Library in New York and we wish to thank its Curator, Fredric Woodbridge Wilson, for his valuable help. Grateful thanks are also due to Albert Truelove, Secretary to Dame Bridget D'Oyly Carte and Manager of the Savoy Theatre, for help and advice on numerous occasions; to Peter Riley, former General Manager of the Company, for his help in getting the project started; and to Margaret Bowden and the Staff of the D'Oyly Carte Office for their encouragement during the many hours we spent working our way through the archives.

Finally we wish to express our grateful thanks to Rick Fawcett, the designer of the book, and to Russell Ash, Beatrice Philpotts, Michael Dover and Linda Doeser for guiding it through from the original proposal to the finished product. Although errors will inevitably occur in a book of this kind, any blame for them must lie on our shoulders, and we should be grateful if they could be brought to our attention. In the meantime, we hope that you will derive as much pleasure from looking at these pictures as we did in discovering them.

April 1984   R J W   F G L

TOP **Robin Wilson as a Yeoman of the Guard in a performance by the Oxford Operatic Society.**

ABOVE **Frederic Lloyd and Dame Bridget D'Oyly Carte present John Reed to H.R.H. the Duke of Edinburgh during the Centenary Season in April 1975.**

ABOVE **Richard D'Oyly Carte (1844–1901); Helen D'Oyly Carte (1852–1913).**

BELOW **Rupert D'Oyly Carte (1876–1948); Dame Bridget D'Oyly Carte, D.B.E. (born 1908).**

The Curtain Rises

George Grossmith as Jack Point in *The Yeomen of the Guard*.

On March 25, 1875 the curtain rose for the first time on a short satire of the legal profession entitled *Trial by Jury*. Although written as an 'after-piece' for Offenbach's *La Périchole*, it soon became the main attraction, surviving even when the Offenbach was withdrawn. But this was not Gilbert and Sullivan's first collaboration. How did the Savoy Operas start?

In the 1860s Gilbert was beginning to establish himself as a successful dramatist and Sullivan was becoming well known as a serious composer, mainly of sacred music. In 1866 Sullivan met F. C. Burnand (later the editor of *Punch*) who asked him to write the music for his one-act operetta, based on Morton's play *Box and Cox*. Sullivan agreed, the name was changed to *Cox and Box* and the piece was completed in a few days. They later collaborated on a full-length opera *The Contrabandista*.

In 1869, Frederic Clay, one of Sullivan's closest friends, collaborated with W. S. Gilbert on a work entitled *Ages Ago*. Clay took Sullivan to one of his rehearsals and so Gilbert and Sullivan met for the first time. Two years later, John Hollingshead, Manager of the Gaiety Theatre, asked Sullivan to write the music for *Thespis*, by Gilbert. This was the first Gilbert and Sullivan opera; it ran for just ten weeks.

Nothing more was heard of the Gilbert and Sullivan partnership until 1875, when Richard D'Oyly Carte, the manager of the Royalty Theatre in Soho, met W. S. Gilbert and commissioned from him the dramatic cantata *Trial by Jury*, suggesting Sullivan as the composer. For some time D'Oyly Carte had wanted to start an English school of comic opera similar to that enjoyed by the French. He had seen *Thespis* and hoped for a great future from the partnership. He was not to be disappointed.

Trial by Jury proved to be a great success at the Royalty Theatre, in the British provinces and later at the Opéra Comique. Encouraged by this, D'Oyly Carte commissioned Gilbert and Sullivan to write a full-length work for the Opéra Comique, of which he was now Manager. The result was *The Sorcerer*, first performed in November 1877. D'Oyly Carte formed the Comedy Opera Company and several distinguished Savoyards made their Gilbert and Sullivan débuts in this production – notably, George Grossmith, Richard Temple and Rutland Barrington.

H.M.S. Pinafore was Gilbert and Sullivan's first major success, although it was nearly a monumental failure owing to a severe heatwave in London in the summer of 1878. Eventually sales picked up, partly resulting from Sullivan's conducting a selection of *Pinafore* tunes at a London Promenade Concert. Soon everyone was 'whistling all the airs from that infernal nonsense *Pinafore*'. To cope with the demand from the provinces, D'Oyly Carte formed two touring companies and sent them around Britain.

After *H.M.S. Pinafore* had been running for 14 months, Richard D'Oyly Carte severed all connections with the directors of the Comedy Opera Company. On July 31, 1879 they brought a gang of roughs to the Opéra Comique and attempted to steal the *Pinafore* scenery while a performance was still in progress. A fight broke out on stage, but the intrusion proved to be unsuccessful; from August 4 the Company became known as Mr D'Oyly Carte's Opera Company.

Although *H.M.S. Pinafore* was earning large royalties in Britain, the '*Pinafore* mania' that swept across the United States yielded nothing, because of the American copyright laws. In addition, some of the American pirated versions of the opera, although described as 'by Gilbert and Sullivan', bore little or no resemblance to the original work. With a new opera on the way, D'Oyly Carte needed to deal with these problems in advance and so took a Company to New York to give authentic performances of *H.M.S. Pinafore* and of the new opera. Meanwhile, the London Company continued to perform at the Opéra Comique.

The new opera, *The Pirates of Penzance*, opened in New York and England almost simultaneously, on December 30 and 31, 1879, thus establishing both the American and British copyrights; the English performance was given in Paignton by a touring *Pinafore* Company visiting Torquay. The New York Company subsequently returned to England and *The Pirates of Penzance* opened at the Opéra Comique on April 3, 1880. After running successfully for over a year it was eventually replaced by *Patience*, a satire on the current aesthetic movement.

By this time the Gilbert and Sullivan operas had become so popular that Richard D'Oyly Carte decided to build a special theatre to present them. This theatre, the Savoy, was the most modern in London and the first theatre in the world to use the newly-invented electric lighting instead of the unpleasant gas lighting to which audiences had become accustomed. On October 10, 1881, *Patience* was transferred to the Savoy Theatre where it ran for a further 408 performances. The Company by this time included Jessie Bond, Leonora Braham, Alice Barnett and Durward Lely.

The next opera was *Iolanthe*, first performed on November 25, 1882. On the opening night Sullivan learned that his brokers had gone bankrupt and that he was penniless.

Gilbert's finest lyrics and many of Sullivan's greatest songs. This was a happy time for Richard D'Oyly Carte: the opera was enjoying a long run, he had recently married his efficient secretary Helen Lenoir (his first wife having died three years earlier), the grand new Savoy Hotel was being completed and the foundation stone was being laid for his great new project, the Royal English Opera House.

The Yeomen of the Guard ran for over a year and was eventually replaced by *The Gondoliers*, one of the happiest and most sparkling of the Gilbert and Sullivan operas and their last great success. By this time George Grossmith and Richard Temple had left the Company, Courtice Pounds and W. H. Denny had joined and Rutland Barrington had returned after a year's absence. *The Gondoliers* had a highly successful run of 554 performances, second only to *The Mikado*, and Her Majesty Queen Victoria honoured the Company by requesting a Command Performance which was held at Windsor Castle on March 6, 1891.

OPPOSITE **'A Society Clown' – a cartoon by 'Spy' (Leslie Ward) in** *Vanity Faire* **(January 21, 1888).**

LEFT **Richard D'Oyly Carte opening the Savoy Theatre – a drawing from** *Entr'Acte* **(October 8, 1881).**

BELOW **Little D'Oyly Carte puts his Pinafore on again – a drawing in** *Entr'Acte* **(June 10, 1899).**

Fortunately, *Iolanthe* was such a success that Sullivan was quickly able to replenish his pockets. It was also during the run of *Iolanthe* that Arthur Sullivan received his knighthood.

On January 5, 1884, Gilbert and Sullivan's only three-act opera received its first performance. *Princess Ida* was based on one of Gilbert's earlier plays – *The Princess* – which in turn was based on a poem by Tennyson. Although it contains some of Sullivan's finest music, it failed to attract audiences and was withdrawn after only 246 performances. As there was no new opera ready to take its place, Richard D'Oyly Carte presented revivals of *Trial by Jury* and *The Sorcerer* and a children's version of *The Pirates of Penzance*.

One reason for the delay in providing an opera to succeed *Princess Ida* was Gilbert's obsession with writing an opera involving a magic lozenge with special powers over all who swallow it. But Sullivan refused to swallow it and Gilbert eventually gave way and sought further inspiration elsewhere. The result was *The Mikado*, the most popular of all the Gilbert and Sullivan operas. It was first performed on March 14, 1885 and ran for almost two years.

After the enormous popularity of *The Mikado*, its successor was bound to suffer by comparison. This indeed happened to *Ruddigore* in spite of the fact that Gilbert considered it his finest libretto and it contains much fine music. Part of the trouble was caused by the original title *Ruddygore* which gave offence to Victorian audiences. *Ruddigore* ran for only 288 performances – a small number by Savoy standards – and was replaced by revivals of *H.M.S. Pinafore, The Pirates of Penzance* and *The Mikado*.

The *Yeomen of The Guard* was first performed on October 3, 1888. It is the most serious – and, for many people, the best – of the operas. It contains some of

OPPOSITE PAGE **By the late 1860s Gilbert and Sullivan were establishing themselves in their respective fields, as indicated by the two playbills shown here.**

ABOVE *Ages Ago*, **by W. S. Gilbert and Frederic Clay, was first performed on November 22, 1869 at the Royal Gallery of Illustration. It was at a rehearsal of this work that Gilbert and Sullivan first met. Seventeen years later, the idea of pictures coming to life resurfaced in** *Ruddigore*.

BELOW *The Contrabandista*, **by F. C. Burnand and Arthur Sullivan, was first performed on December 18, 1867 at St. George's Opera House, London. A revised version, entitled** *The Chieftain*, **was presented at the Savoy Theatre in 1894 (see page 59).**

THIS PAGE *Thespis*

Thespis, or The Gods Grown Old, **an 'entirely original Grotesque Opera in Two Acts', was Gilbert and Sullivan's first collaboration. It was first performed on December 26, 1871 at the Gaiety Theatre, London, and tells the story of a troupe of actors who climb Mount Olympus and change positions with the gods who have grown old and powerless.**

ABOVE *Here's a pretty tale for future*
Iliads and Odysseys:
Mortals are about to personate
the gods and goddesses.

A drawing from the *Illustrated London News* **(January 6, 1872). Thespis (J. L. Toole) agrees with Jupiter to exchange positions and let the aged gods visit earth for a year. Apollo (Fred Sullivan), Mars (Frank Wood) and Mercury (Nellie Farren, right) look on.**

LEFT **A programme from the original run of** *Thespis*.

Trial by Jury, a 'novel and entirely original Dramatic Cantata', was first performed on March 25, 1875 at the Royalty Theatre, London. It was commissioned by Richard D'Oyly Carte, the manager of the theatre, to complete a triple bill with Offenbach's *La Périchole*, starring the theatre's owner Mme. Selina Dolaro, and a farce entitled *Cryptoconchoid-syphonostomata*, and soon became the evening's main attraction. Written and rehearsed in three weeks, it tells the story of a case of Breach of Promise.

OPPOSITE *When I, good friends, was called to the bar, I'd an appetite fresh and hearty . . .*
Frederic Sullivan, the composer's brother, as the Learned Judge. During the run of *Trial by Jury*, he fell ill and died at the age of 39. *The Lost Chord* was written as he lay dying.

INSET The first night programme for *Trial by Jury*, depicting Gilbert and Sullivan cherubs, a picture of Selina Dolaro and a scene from *La Périchole*.

ABOVE *That she is reeling is plain to see!*
A drawing from *The Illustrated Sporting and Dramatic News* (May 1, 1875) of a scene from *Trial by Jury*.

LEFT W. S. Penley as the Foreman of the Jury. He subsequently was to create the rôle of Charley in *Charley's Aunt*.

The Sorcerer, the first full-length Gilbert and Sullivan opera commissioned by Richard D'Oyly Carte, was first performed on November 17, 1877 at the Opéra Comique.

OPPOSITE PAGE **Two contemporary drawings of the original production.**

ABOVE *What is this fairy form I see before me?* **Lady Sangazure, having drunk the philtre, is immediately attracted to John Wellington Wells.**

BELOW **The Incantation Scene, in which John Wellington Wells mixes the potion.**

THIS PAGE **Three distinguished Savoyards made their Gilbert and Sullivan débuts in *The Sorcerer*.**

ABOVE LEFT **George Grossmith as John Wellington Wells, of J. W. Wells & Co., Family Sorcerers. He was a member of the Company from 1877 to 1889 and created most of the comedy rôles.**

ABOVE *I'm your servant most attentive . . .* **Richard Temple as Sir Marmaduke Pointdextre with Mrs. Howard Paul as Lady Sangazure. He was a member of the Company from 1877 to 1889, and in the 1890s, and created most of the 'Mikado rôles'.**

LEFT **Rutland Barrington as Dr. Daly. He was a member of the Company from 1877 to 1888, 1889 to 1896 and 1908 to 1909, and created most of the 'Pooh-Bah rôles'.**

H.M.S. Pinafore, **or** *The Lass that Loved a Sailor,* **an 'entirely original Nautical Comic Opera in Two Acts', was first performed on May 25, 1878 at the Opéra Comique. It tells the story of Ralph Rackstraw, a seaman on board H.M.S. Pinafore, who loves Josephine, the Captain's daughter. The opera was so successful that D'Oyly Carte presented a** *Children's Pinafore* **in which all the parts were played by children aged between 10 and 13 years.**

FAR LEFT ABOVE **A drawing from the** *Illustrated London News* **(June 8, 1878) depicting the scene in which Captain Corcoran discovers Ralph eloping with Josephine.**

FAR LEFT BELOW **From left to right: Richard Temple as Dick Deadeye, George Power as Ralph Rackstraw and George Grossmith as Sir Joseph Porter, K.C.B.**

ABOVE **A drawing from the** *Illustrated London News* **(January 17, 1880) featuring the** *Children's Pinafore.*

LEFT **A** *Pinafore* **programme with an announcement of the first performance of the** *Children's Pinafore.*

The Pirates of Penzance, **or** *The Slave of Duty,* **was given its British and American premières on December 30 and 31, 1879 at the Royal Bijou Theatre, Paignton (to establish the British copyright), and the Fifth Avenue Theatre, New York (to establish the American copyright). After a run in New York, it was transferred to the Opéra Comique, London, in April 1880.**

ABOVE TOP **The Fifth Avenue Theatre, New York.**

ABOVE **A poster advertising the copyright performance at the Royal Bijou Theatre, Paignton.**

CENTRE *A nurserymaid is not afraid*
of what you people call work,
So I made up my mind to go as a kind
of piratical maid-of-all-work.
Alice Barnett, who created the rôle of Ruth in the
New York production. She was a large woman, six
feet tall with a figure to match, who later created the
rôles of Lady Jane and the Queen of the Fairies.

ABOVE Three photographs of the original London
cast: Richard Temple (top left) as the Pirate King;
Rutland Barrington (top right) as the Sergeant of
Police; and Marion Hood as Mabel. In the New York
production, the Pirate King and the Sergeant of
Police were given the names Richard and Edward.

ACT. I

"I AM A PIRATE "KING""

"I AM THE VERY MODEL OF A MODERN MAJOR GENERAL"

"A POLICEMAN'S LOT IS NOT A HAPPY ONE"

"TAKE ANY HEART TAKE MINE"

OPPOSITE **Two drawings of** *The Pirates of Penzance* **from** *The Illustrated Sporting and Dramatic News,* **depicting the Act 1 Finale and the 'paradox trio'.**

ABOVE **In 1884 Richard D'Oyly Carte presented a** *Children's Pirates* **at the Savoy Theatre, in which all the parts were played by children aged 10–13.**

"We are indeed jolly utter"
"Patience, or Bunthornes Bride"

Richd Temple
Frank T. Thornton
Durward Lely

Patience, **or** Bunthorne's Bride, **a 'new and original Aesthetic Opera in Two Acts', was first performed on April 23, 1881 at the Opéra Comique. Intended as a satire on the aesthetic movement of Oscar Wilde, it tells the story of Bunthorne, a poet who is madly loved by a bevy of love-sick maidens but whose fancy has turned towards Patience, a dairy maid.**

OPPOSITE PAGE

ABOVE LEFT *There will be too much of me*
In the coming by-and-by!
Alice Barnett as the Lady Jane.

ABOVE RIGHT **Frank Thornton as Major Murgatroyd.**

BELOW *In a doleful train*
Two and two we walk all day –
A drawing from Society **(May 7, 1881). The love-sick maidens have deserted Bunthorne and sworn allegiance to his rival, the idyllic poet Archibald Grosvenor.**

THIS PAGE

ABOVE **George Grossmith walks his flowery way as Reginald Bunthorne, a fleshly poet.**

ABOVE LEFT **Leonora Braham in the title rôle. She was a member of the Company from 1881 to 1887 and created several of the soprano rôles.**

LEFT **Richard Temple, Durward Lely and Frank Thornton as the three aesthetic dragoons in Act 2.**

27

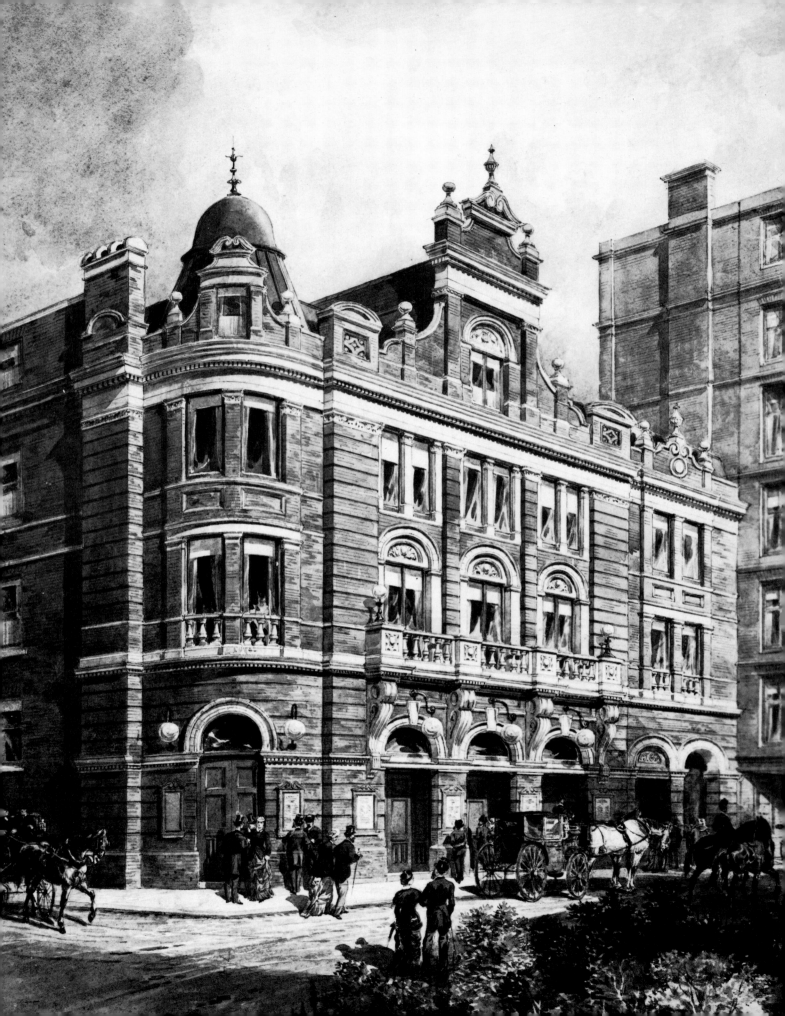

On October 10, 1881 Richard D'Oyly Carte's dream came true. The Savoy Theatre, built for the performance of the Gilbert and Sullivan operas, opened in a blaze of publicity with a gala performance of *Patience*, transferred from the Opéra Comique.

The Savoy Theatre was the most modern theatre in London. Beautifully decorated in white, pale yellow and gold with Venetian red boxes and dark blue seats, and with a gold satin curtain instead of the usual printed act-drop, it was a model of taste, safety and comfort. Most important of all, it was the first public building in the world to be lit throughout by electricity. On the opening night the audience gasped and then cheered, as the auditorium gas lights (installed for safety) were lowered to make way for the soft soothing light of 1,200 electric lamps. Other innovations introduced by Richard D'Oyly Carte were the queueing system for tickets (queues were previously unknown), a no-tipping rule for attendants, free programmes, properly printed instead of the usual crudely-printed playbills, and proper whisky in the bars.

OPPOSITE The original façade of the Savoy Theatre, facing the Embankment.

ABOVE A drawing from the *Graphic* (December 17, 1881), showing a scene from Act 1 of *Patience* on the opening night. The electric lights around the auditorium can be clearly seen.

LEFT The circular foyer of the Savoy Theatre.

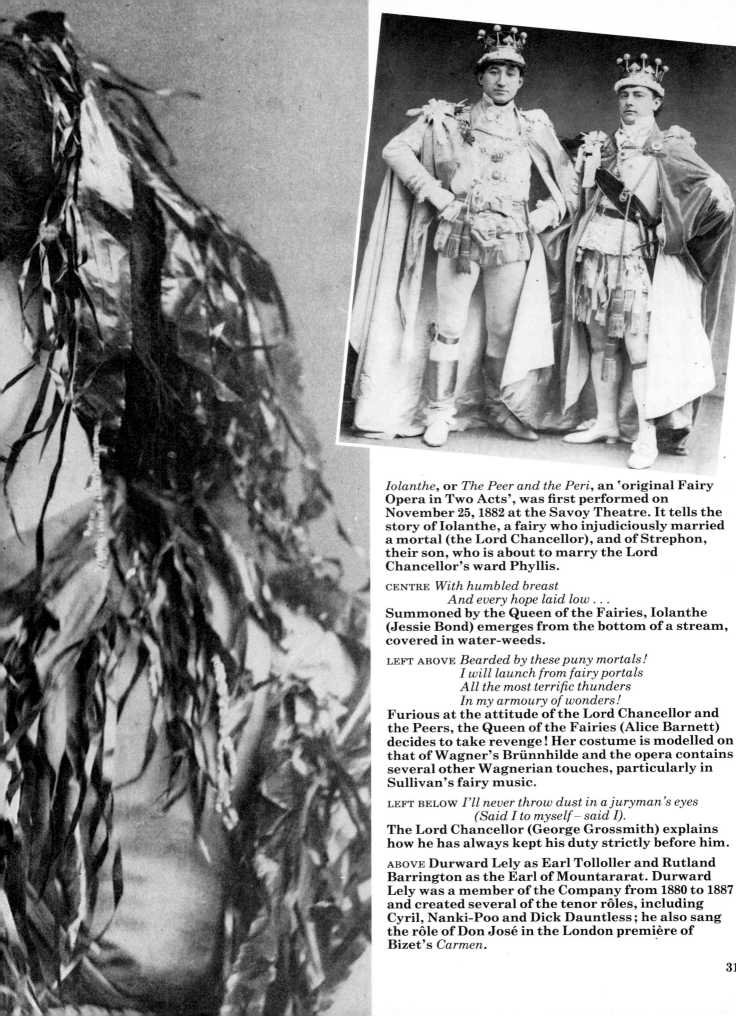

Iolanthe, or *The Peer and the Peri*, an 'original Fairy Opera in Two Acts', was first performed on November 25, 1882 at the Savoy Theatre. It tells the story of Iolanthe, a fairy who injudiciously married a mortal (the Lord Chancellor), and of Strephon, their son, who is about to marry the Lord Chancellor's ward Phyllis.

CENTRE *With humbled breast*
And every hope laid low . . .
Summoned by the Queen of the Fairies, Iolanthe (Jessie Bond) emerges from the bottom of a stream, covered in water-weeds.

LEFT ABOVE *Bearded by these puny mortals!*
I will launch from fairy portals
All the most terrific thunders
In my armoury of wonders!
Furious at the attitude of the Lord Chancellor and the Peers, the Queen of the Fairies (Alice Barnett) decides to take revenge! Her costume is modelled on that of Wagner's Brünnhilde and the opera contains several other Wagnerian touches, particularly in Sullivan's fairy music.

LEFT BELOW *I'll never throw dust in a juryman's eyes*
(Said I to myself – said I).
The Lord Chancellor (George Grossmith) explains how he has always kept his duty strictly before him.

ABOVE Durward Lely as Earl Tolloller and Rutland Barrington as the Earl of Mountararat. Durward Lely was a member of the Company from 1880 to 1887 and created several of the tenor rôles, including Cyril, Nanki-Poo and Dick Dauntless; he also sang the rôle of Don José in the London première of Bizet's *Carmen*.

31

Princess Ida

Princess Ida, **or** *Castle Adamant*, **was described by W. S. Gilbert as 'a respectful Operatic Per-Version of Tennyson's** *The Princess* **in a Prologue and Two Acts'. It was first performed on January 5, 1884 at the Savoy Theatre, and tells the story of Prince Hilarion's attempts to woo Princess Ida who runs a women's college at Castle Adamant and to whom he was betrothed in infancy.**

OPPOSITE *Isn't your life extremely flat*
With nothing whatever to grumble at.
George Grossmith as King Gama.

LEFT *Now hearken to my strict command*
King Hildebrand (Rutland Barrington) instructs his Court as to how King Gama should be treated.

BELOW **From left to right: Durward Lely as Cyril, a friend of Hilarion; Rosina Brandram as Lady Blanche, Professor of Abstract Science; and Leonora Braham in the title rôle. Rosina Brandram was a member of the Company from 1878 to 1903 and created many of the contralto rôles.**

ABOVE TOP **A drawing from** *The Illustrated Sporting and Dramatic News* **(January 19, 1884) showing King Hildebrand's arrival at Castle Adamant.**

ABOVE **A Schweppes advertisement from the** *Princess Ida* **programme.**

RIGHT *We are warriors three – Sons of Gama, Rex.* **King Gama's three sons, Arac, Guron and Scynthius (Richard Temple, Warwick Gray and William Lugg).**

After the short run of *Princess Ida* (246 performances), there was no new Gilbert and Sullivan opera to take its place. To fill the gap, Richard D'Oyly Carte presented revivals of *Trial by Jury* and *The Sorcerer*, as well as a Children's version of *The Pirates of Penzance* (see page 25).

The Sorcerer

ABOVE LEFT A Savoy Theatre programme for the 1884–85 revival of *The Sorcerer*.

ABOVE *Ye fiends of night, your filthy blight*
In noisome plenty yield!
John Wellington Wells (George Grossmith), holding the teapot aloft prepares the love philtre for the villagers of Ploverleigh.

Trial by Jury

LEFT *In Westminster Hall I danced a dance,*
Like a semi-despondent fury.
Rutland Barrington as the Learned Judge. An unusual feature of this revival was the final 'transformation scene' in which the Judge and the Plaintiff became Harlequin and Columbine and the curtain fell amidst red fire and flames.

The Mikado, **or** *The Town of Titipu*, **an 'entirely original Japanese Opera in Two Acts', was first performed on March 14, 1885 at the Savoy Theatre. The most popular of all Gilbert and Sullivan operas, it tells the story of Nanki-Poo, a wandering minstrel in love with Yum-Yum, the ward of Ko-Ko.**

OPPOSITE *Behold the Lord High Executioner!*
    A personage of noble rank and title –
    A dignified and potent officer . . .
George Grossmith as Ko-Ko, the Lord High Executioner of Titipu.

INSET *I tune my supple song!*
Durward Lely as Nanki-Poo, the son of the Mikado, disguised as a wandering minstrel.

ABOVE *From every kind of man*
    Obedience I expect;
    I'm the Emperor of Japan –
Two portrayals of the title rôle – Richard Temple (left) who created the rôle at the Savoy Theatre, and F. Federici (right) who played it in New York.

RIGHT **Rutland Barrington as Pooh-Bah, the haughty and exclusive Lord High Everything Else.**

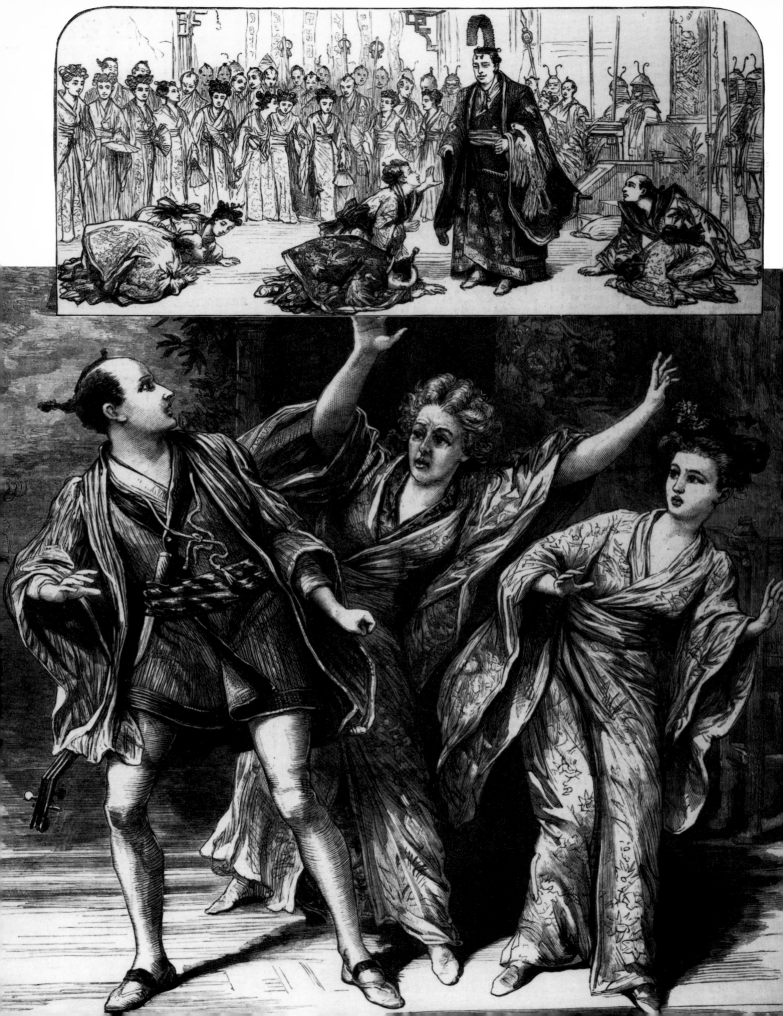

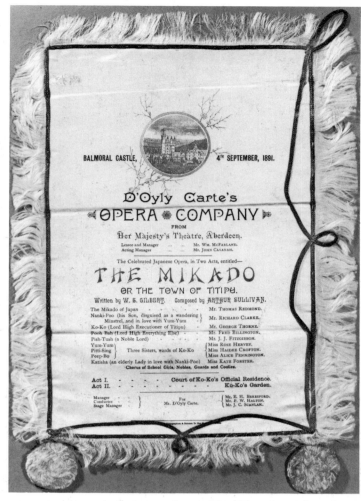

OPPOSITE PAGE **A drawing from** *The Illustrated Sporting and Dramatic News* **of two scenes from** *The Mikado.*

ABOVE **The Mikado tells Pitti-Sing, Ko-Ko and Pooh-Bah that the punishment for compassing the death of the Heir Apparent is 'something lingering with boiling oil in it'.**

BELOW *I'll tear the mask from your disguising!* **Katisha's dramatic entrance during the Finale of Act 1 when she threatens to reveal the true identity of Nanki-Poo, the son of the Mikado.**

THIS PAGE

ABOVE LEFT *I mean to rule the earth,*
   As he the sky –
  We really know our worth,
   The sun and I!
Leonora Braham as Yum-Yum, admired by Sybil Grey and Jessie Bond as Peep-Bo and Pitti-Sing.

LEFT **Sybil Grey, Leonora Braham and Jessie Bond meet for a reunion in London on March 14, 1930 – 45 years after the first performance.**

ABOVE **Although the London run of** *The Mikado* **ended in January 1887, the D'Oyly Carte touring companies continued to present it in the provinces. On September 4, 1891, one of these touring companies gave a Royal Command Performance of the opera at Balmoral Castle.**

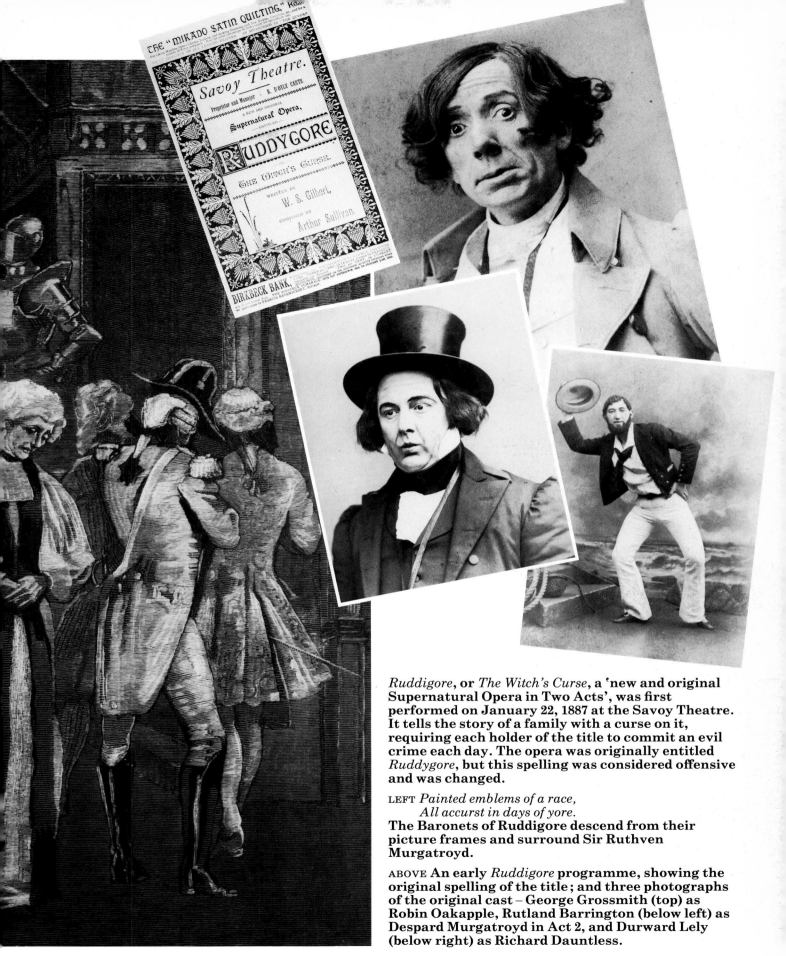

Ruddigore, or *The Witch's Curse*, a 'new and original Supernatural Opera in Two Acts', was first performed on January 22, 1887 at the Savoy Theatre. It tells the story of a family with a curse on it, requiring each holder of the title to commit an evil crime each day. The opera was originally entitled *Ruddygore*, but this spelling was considered offensive and was changed.

LEFT *Painted emblems of a race,*
All accurst in days of yore.
The Baronets of Ruddigore descend from their picture frames and surround Sir Ruthven Murgatroyd.

ABOVE An early *Ruddigore* programme, showing the original spelling of the title; and three photographs of the original cast – George Grossmith (top) as Robin Oakapple, Rutland Barrington (below left) as Despard Murgatroyd in Act 2, and Durward Lely (below right) as Richard Dauntless.

41

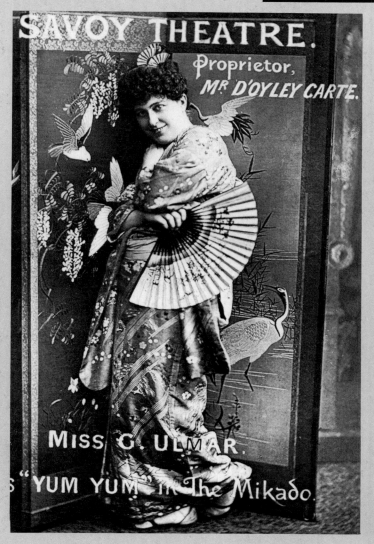

OPPOSITE PAGE *Ruddigore*

ABOVE *To a garden full of posies*
Cometh one to gather flowers.
Jessie Bond as poor Mad Margaret.

BELOW **Two portrayals of Rose Maybud – Leonora Braham (right) who created the part and Geraldine Ulmar (left) who replaced her.**

THIS PAGE

After the relatively short run of *Ruddigore* **(288 performances) there was no new Gilbert and Sullivan opera to take its place. To fill the gap, Richard D'Oyly Carte presented revivals of** *H.M.S. Pinafore*, *The Pirates of Penzance* **and** *The Mikado*.

ABOVE LEFT *Come of your Buttercup buy!*
Rosina Brandram as Little Buttercup, a Portsmouth Bumboat Woman, in the 1887 *H.M.S. Pinafore* **revival.**

LEFT **A drawing from** *The Illustrated Sporting and Dramatic News* **showing the elaborate set for the 1887 revival of** *H.M.S. Pinafore*, **with a real deck laid on stage and the yardarms manned by sailors.**

ABOVE **An advertisement for the 1888 revival of** *The Mikado*, **featuring Geraldine Ulmar as Yum-Yum.**

43

Phoebe Meryll (Miss Jessie Bond) and Wilfred Shadbolt (Mr. W. H. Denny) 'Were I thy Bride'

The Yeomen of the Guard, or *The Merryman and his Maid*, a 'new and original Opera in Two Acts', was first performed on October 3, 1888 at the Savoy Theatre. More serious than all the other Gilbert and Sullivan operas, it tells the story of Colonel Fairfax, under sentence of death in the Tower of London, and of his escape and marriage to Elsie Maynard, a Strolling Singer.

ABOVE LEFT **Courtice Pounds as Jack Point, a rôle he played with a D'Oyly Carte touring company. He was a member of the Company from 1882 to 1892 and created the rôles of Colonel Fairfax and Marco Palmieri.**

ABOVE **Courtice Pounds as Colonel Fairfax. Having been rescued from his cell by Sergeant Meryll, Fairfax assumes the rôle of his son Leonard Meryll who has just been appointed a Yeoman of the Guard.**

LEFT **A drawing from the *Graphic* (October 13, 1888). Colonel Fairfax, under sentence of death for sorcery, greets his old friend Sir Richard Cholmondeley, the Lieutenant of the Tower, watched by Sergeant Meryll and Phoebe.**

OPPOSITE **The Headsman and his two Assistants.**

The Yeomen of the Guard

ABOVE
Were I thy bride,
Then all the world beside
Were not too wide
   To hold my wealth of love –
Were I thy bride!

**Phoebe Meryll (Jessie Bond) distracts the attention
of the Head Jailer Wilfred Shadbolt (W. H. Denny) as
she slyly borrows his keys to open Colonel Fairfax's
cell. Jessie Bond was a member of the Company from
1878 to 1891 and in 1895 and 1896. She created most of
the leading soubrette rôles, starting with Cousin
Hebe and including Iolanthe, Pitti-Sing and Tessa.
William Denny was a member of the Company from
1888 to 1894 and created the rôles of Wilfred
Shadbolt, Don Alhambra del Bolero and Scaphio.**

RIGHT **A Savoy Theatre programme for 1889, showing
Phoebe Meryll at her spinning wheel.**

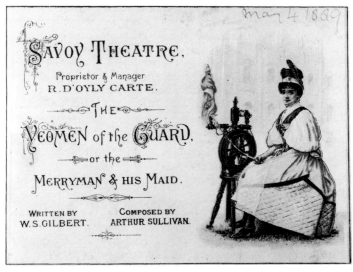

The Gondoliers, **or** *The King of Barataria*, **an 'entirely original Comic Opera in Two Acts', was first performed on December 7, 1889 at the Savoy Theatre. It tells the story of two Venetian Gondoliers, Marco and Giuseppe, one of whom is believed to be the only son of the late King of Barataria and to have been married in infancy to Casilda, the daughter of the Duke and Duchess of Plaza-Toro.**

ABOVE *That very knowing, overflowing,*
Easy-going Paladin,
The Duke of Plaza-Toro.
Frank Wyatt as the Duke of Plaza-Toro, a Grandee of Spain.

RIGHT *Replying, we sing*
As one individual . . .
Giuseppe and Marco Palmieri (Rutland Barrington and Courtice Pounds) decide to rule Barataria jointly until it is determined which of them is King.

The Gondoliers

RIGHT *Try we life-long, we can never*
Straighten out life's tangled skein.
A contemporary drawing from the *Graphic* (December 14, 1889) of the quintet from Act 1.

BELOW Four members of the original cast: Courtice Pounds as Marco Palmieri in his Act 2 costume as one of the Kings of Barataria; W. H. Denny as Don Alhambra del Bolero, the Grand Inquisitor of Spain; and Wallace Brownlow and Decima Moore as Luiz and Casilda, the eventual King and Queen of Barataria. (Decima Moore created this rôle when she was only 18 years old.)

On March 6, 1891, the Company performed *The Gondoliers* at Windsor Castle in the presence of Her Majesty Queen Victoria, The Prince and Princess of Wales and other members of the Royal Family. The performance was such a success that another Royal Command Performance took place later in the same year – *The Mikado*, presented by a D'Oyly Carte touring company at Balmoral Castle on September 4, 1891 (see page 39).

ABOVE TOP The set for Act 2 of *The Gondoliers* in the Waterloo Chamber at Windsor Castle. Eighty-six years later, on June 16, 1977, another D'Oyly Carte performance took place in the same Chamber (see page 185).

ABOVE A contemporary drawing from the *Daily Graphic* (March 9, 1891) of Her Majesty Queen Victoria enjoying the quintet from Act 1 with the Duke and Duchess of Edinburgh, the Duke and Duchess of Connaught, Prince and Princess Christian and Princess Beatrice.

Early Days

Walter Passmore as the Devil in *The Beauty Stone*

The early successes of the Savoy Operas were too good to last. The year 1890 saw the beginning of the end with the famous 'carpet quarrel', after which nothing was ever the same. Richard D'Oyly Carte had bought new carpets for the front of the house and (as with other expenses) had divided the cost among the three of them. Gilbert considered this an unnecessary expense and challenged him. Sullivan sided with D'Oyly Carte, the arguments became very bitter, Gilbert refused permission for his operas to be performed at the Savoy and the matter ended up in the Law Courts. A settlement was eventually reached and the partners finally shook hands, but the damage had been done by then.

In the following year Richard D'Oyly Carte had other problems. He had intended his Royal English Opera House to be a permanent home for British opera and had opened it in grand style with Arthur Sullivan's new opera *Ivanhoe*, written partly at the suggestion of Her Majesty Queen Victoria. Unfortunately, *Ivanhoe* lasted only 155 performances – a good number for a grand opera, but far below D'Oyly Carte's expectations. With nothing to follow *Ivanhoe*, except a comic opera by Messager, he was forced to sell the Opera House and see it eventually turned into a music hall.

Meanwhile, back at the Savoy, several new operas were being introduced to the public – in particular, *The Nautch Girl*, *The Vicar of Bray*, *Haddon Hall* and *Jane Annie* (see pages 54–55). Eventually, in October 1893, a new Gilbert and Sullivan opera was ready – *Utopia Limited*, the most lavishly presented of all. The first performance went well, but the old spark had gone and the opera lasted only 245 performances. It was succeeded in 1894 by *Mirette* and *The Chieftain*, the latter being a revised version by Burnand and Sullivan of their earlier opera *The Contrabandista*.

After *The Chieftain*, the Company toured the London suburbs while the Carl Rosa Opera Company occupied the Savoy. The theatre was then closed for several months until November 1895, when a revival of *The Mikado* took place. This was highly successful, with Rutland Barrington and Jessie Bond returning to join the 'new Savoyards', Walter Passmore, R. Scott Fishe, Charles Kenningham, Emmie Owen and Florence Perry.

Meanwhile, the next and last Gilbert and Sullivan opera was in preparation. On March 7, 1896 the curtain rose on *The Grand Duke*, their final collaboration. Its opening night was a triumph, as always, but it failed to catch on and fizzled out after only 123 performances. *The Mikado* was resurrected and ran for a further seven months.

For the next seven years, new operas were interspersed with Gilbert and Sullivan revivals. *His Majesty* gave way to a revival of *The Yeomen of the Guard*, which in turn was replaced by Offenbach's *The Grand Duchess of Gerolstein* and *The Gondoliers*. The new operas presented were *The Beauty Stone*, *The Lucky Star* and *The Rose of Persia* (see pages 66–67), and the revivals were *Trial by Jury*, *The Sorcerer*, *H.M.S. Pinafore*, *The Pirates of Penzance* and *Patience*.

During the *Patience* revival of 1900–01, three important deaths occurred – Sir Arthur Sullivan's in November 1900, Her Majesty Queen Victoria's in January 1901 and Richard D'Oyly Carte's in April 1901. Gilbert, Sullivan and D'Oyly Carte had all intended to appear on stage on the opening night of the *Patience* revival, but Sullivan was already dying and only Gilbert and D'Oyly Carte were able be there.

After Richard D'Oyly Carte's death, his wife took over the Savoy Theatre and subsequently sold it to William Greet. During Greet's period in office, *Iolanthe* was revived for the first time and the Company introduced several new operas, including *The Emerald Isle* and *Merrie England*. After a three-month tour, the Company returned to the Savoy to perform *The Princess of Kensington* by Basil Hood and Edward German.

In May 1903 the Company went on tour and did not return to central London for more than three years. Most of the touring was in the British provinces, but in December 1904 the Company left for a seven-month tour of South Africa.

The first D'Oyly Carte repertory season took place at the Savoy Theatre from December 1906 to August 1907, and was a sensation. New productions of four operas were presented (see pages 82–85), under the direction of W. S. Gilbert and J. M. Gordon. The season concluded with an extended last night, starting at 4 p.m. and containing an act from each of the four operas. Also included was a scene from *The Mikado*, an opera which was banned from the Savoy during 1907, but which continued to play in the provinces (see page 83).

The first repertory season was such a success that Helen D'Oyly Carte presented a second season at the Savoy Theatre from April 1908 to March 1909. Six operas were presented, and Rutland Barrington and Richard Temple returned to play some of their original rôles. As with the first repertory season, the performances were enthusiastically received. After this season, Helen D'Oyly Carte retired. The Company went on tour in the British provinces, and it did not return to central London for ten years.

RIGHT **The Royal English Opera House in Cambridge Circus, London was built by Richard D'Oyly Carte to stage English Grand Opera. It opened on January 31, 1891 with** *Ivanhoe*, **a 'Romantic Grand Opera in Three Acts' with a libretto by Julian Sturgis and music by Sir Arthur Sullivan. Several members of the cast were former or future members of the D'Oyly Carte Company.** *Ivanhoe* **had two alternating casts and ran for 155 consecutive performances – a record for a Grand Opera. Unfortunately, D'Oyly Carte had expected a much longer run and had no ready successor except André Messager's light opera** *La Basoche* **which ran for only ten weeks. Disillusioned, he sold the building which then became a music hall. It is now the Palace Theatre.**

ABOVE **Charles Kenningham as Maurice de Bracy. He was a member of the Company from 1891 to 1898.**

ABOVE RIGHT **Richard Green as Prince John.**

OPPOSITE **'Royal English Opera' – a cartoon by Spy (Leslie Ward) in** *Vanity Fair* **(February 14, 1891).**

When *The Gondoliers* finished its run in June 1891, there were no new Gilbert and Sullivan operas to take its place and various other works were presented. The first of these was *The Nautch Girl*, or *The Rajah of Chutneypore*, a comic opera by George Dance and Frank Desprez with music by Edward Solomon; it ran from June 1891 to January 1892. This was followed by *The Vicar of Bray*, a revised version of a comic opera by Sydney Grundy and Edward Solomon which had first been presented in 1882. The next production was *Haddon Hall*, a 'light English opera' by Sydney Grundy and Sir Arthur Sullivan, which ran from September 1892 to April 1893 and which gave way to *Jane Annie*, a comic opera by J. M. Barrie and Arthur Conan Doyle in which Walter Passmore made his D'Oyly Carte début.

OPPOSITE PAGE *The Vicar of Bray* Rutland Barrington as the Rev. William Barlow, the Vicar of Bray.

INSET *The Vicar of Bray* Louise Rowe as Cynthia, a lady teacher.

THIS PAGE

ABOVE LEFT *The Nautch Girl* Rutland Barrington as Punka, the Rajah of Chutneypore.

LEFT *The Nautch Girl* W. H. Denny as Bumbo, an Idol.

ABOVE *Haddon Hall* Richard Green as Sir George Vernon, a Royalist.

Utopia (Limited), **or** *The Flowers of Progress*, **an 'Original Comic opera in Two Acts' was first performed on October 7, 1893 at the Savoy Theatre. Now usually written as** *Utopia Limited*, **it tells the story of a tropical island ruled by King Paramount and of its attempts to become Anglicized when his daughter Zara returns to the island after five years in England, bringing with her six 'Flowers of Progress' – experts in various aspects of English life. It was the first Gilbert and Sullivan opera since the 'carpet quarrel', and achieved a run of only 245 performances. Attempts were made to revive it in the 1920s, but it was not performed again by the Company until 1975.**

OPPOSITE *Let all your doubts take wing –*
Our influence is great.
W. H. Denny as Scaphio, a Judge of the Utopian Supreme Court.

ABOVE **W. S. Gilbert reads the libretto of** *Utopia Limited* **to the assembled Company at the Savoy Theatre. From left to right: F. Cellier (Musical Director), W. S. Gilbert, Sir Arthur Sullivan, Helen and Richard D'Oyly Carte, W. H. Denny, Emmie Owen, Florence Perry, Charles Harris (Stage Director), W. H. Seymour (Stage Manager), Rutland Barrington, Rosina Brandram, Nancy McIntosh, Lawrence Gridley, Charles Kenningham, R. Scott Fishe and Walter Passmore.**

LEFT *Lalabalele talala! Callabale lalabalica*
falahle! Callamalala galalate! . . .
Walter Passmore as Tarara, the Public Exploder. Tarara is in great rage and angrily lets off steam in the Utopian language. (Tarara-BOOM-de-ay was the current popular song in 1893.)

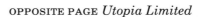

OPPOSITE PAGE *Utopia Limited*

ABOVE **The Flowers of Progress, ranged across the stage as Christy Minstrels.**

BELOW LEFT **Rosina Brandram as Lady Sophy, an English Gouvernante, with Princesses Nekaya and Kalyba (Emmie Owen and Florence Perry), daughters of King Paramount.**

BELOW RIGHT *Ah, do not laugh at my attempted C!* **Captain Fitzbattleaxe (Charles Kenningham) complains that the fervour of his love for Princess Zara (Nancy McIntosh) is affecting his singing voice.**

THIS PAGE *The Chieftain*

In December 1894 Richard D'Oyly Carte presented *The Chieftain*, a comic opera by F. C. Burnand and Arthur Sullivan. It was a re-working of *The Contrabandista* (see page 14) and ran for only 97 performances.

LEFT **Dudley Hardy's striking poster for the opera.**

BELOW **R. Scott Fishe (left) as Ferdinand, the Chieftain of the Ladrones, and Walter Passmore (right) as Peter A. Grigg, a British tourist in search of the picturesque.**

The Grand Duke, or *The Statutory Duel*, was first performed on March 7, 1896 at the Savoy Theatre. It tells the story of a theatrical company that is plotting to overthrow the despotic Grand Duke Rudolph and take his place. Rudolph is about to be married to the Baroness von Krakenfeldt, but was betrothed in infancy to the Princess of Monte Carlo who turns up at the end of the opera.

The opera had a very successful first night, but the enthusiasm quickly waned. Although the score contains two or three excellent songs, the work is very weak in places and the opera was withdrawn after only 123 performances. It was never revived by the Company, except for a concert performance in 1975 and a recording issued in 1976.

ABOVE The set for Act 1, the market-place of the town of Speisesaal in the Grand Duchy of Pfennig Halbpfennig in the year 1750. It was designed by W. Harford and was much praised by the critics.

RIGHT A poster for *The Grand Duke* by Dudley Hardy (1867–1922), a painter, illustrator and designer of posters and magazine advertisements. He designed several striking posters for the Company, including ones for *The Chieftain* (on page 59) and *The Yeomen of the Guard* (in the title pages).

OPPOSITE *Observe! My snuff-box!*
Walter Passmore as Rudolph, the stingy and dyspeptic Grand Duke of Pfennig Halbpfennig. He was a member of the Company from 1893 to 1903, making his début in *Jane Annie* and proceeding via Tarara in *Utopia Limited* to the main comedy rôles.

"THE GRAND DUKE."

BY
W·S·GILBERT
AND
ARTHUR SULLIVAN

SAVOY THEATRE·
Proprietor & Manager, R. D'OYLY CARTE.

CENTRE *We're rigged out in magnificent array*
R. Scott Fishe as the Prince of Monte Carlo.

LEFT ABOVE **Jones Hewson as the Herald and C. H. Workman as Ben Hashbaz, the Court Costumier. The Herald's solo introducing the Prince and Princess of Monte Carlo at the end of Act 2 was an unexpected highlight of the first performance.**

LEFT BELOW **Emmie Owen as the Princess of Monte Carlo, who was betrothed in infancy to the Grand Duke Rudolph and arrives to claim him at the end of the opera.**

ABOVE *How would I play this part –*
The Grand Duke's Bride?
Ilka von Palmay as Julia Jellicoe, an English comedienne. She was a Hungarian soprano whose Gilbert and Sullivan appearances had included the role of Nanki-Poo in *The Mikado* in Berlin! In the D'Oyly Carte she also played the rôle of Elsie Maynard in *The Yeomen of the Guard*.

Revivals of *The Mikado* and *The Yeomen of the Guard* took place at the Savoy Theatre during the years 1895 to 1897.

THIS PAGE *The Mikado*

ABOVE **Walter Passmore (left) as Ko-Ko, and R. Scott Fishe (right) as the Mikado.**

LEFT **Charles Kenningham as Nanki-Poo and Florence Perry as Yum-Yum flout the law by flirting in public.**

OPPOSITE **The original playbills for *Cox and Box*, at the Royal Gallery of Illustration in 1869, and *H.M.S Pinafore*, at the Opéra Comique in 1878.**

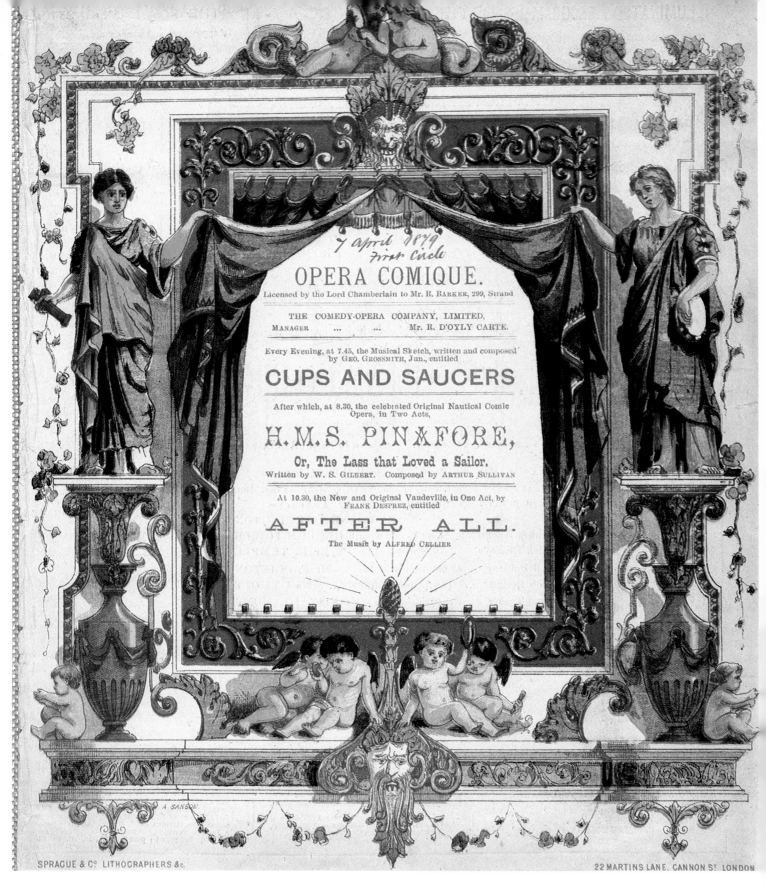

7 april 1879
First Circle

OPERA COMIQUE.

Licensed by the Lord Chamberlain to Mr. R. BARKER, 299, Strand

THE COMEDY-OPERA COMPANY, LIMITED,

MANAGER ... ... Mr. R. D'OYLY CARTE.

Every Evening, at 7.45, the Musical Sketch, written and composed by GEO. GROSSMITH, Jun., entitled

CUPS AND SAUCERS

After which, at 8.30, the celebrated Original Nautical Comic Opera, in Two Acts,

H.M.S. PINAFORE,

Or, The Lass that Loved a Sailor.

Written by W. S. GILBERT. Composed by ARTHUR SULLIVAN

At 10.30, the New and Original Vaudeville, in One Act, by FRANK DESPREZ, entitled

AFTER ALL.

The Music by ALFRED CELLIER

SPRAGUE & Cº. LITHOGRAPHERS &c.

22 MARTINS LANE, CANNON Sᵗ. LONDON

ABOVE **The programme for a performance of** *H.M.S. Pinafore* **at the Opéra Comique on April 7, 1879. It was performed with two other works, one of which was written and composed by George Grossmith.**

OPPOSITE **The programme for a performance of** *Patience* **at the Savoy Theatre on October 17, 1881, one week after the theatre opened. The inside of the programme contains further scenes from the opera.**

SAVOY THEATRE

Sole Proprietor &
Manager
R. D'Oyly Carte

PATIENCE

By

W. S. GILBERT

AND

ARTHUR SULLIVAN

GILBERT

TRIAL by JURY
The SORCERER
H.M.S. PINAFORE
The PIRATES of PENZANCE
PATIENCE
IOLANTHE
PRINCESS IDA

Henry Michael Brock (1875–1960) was an illustrator and a water-colour artist who contributed drawings to *Punch*, *Graphic*, *The Sketch* and several other magazines. This picture, sometimes entitled *Over the Moon*, features over 60 characters from nine of the Gilbert and Sullivan operas. It was designed for the front cover of the programmes for the 1919–20 season at the Princes Theatre, London. The *Iolanthe*, *Patience* and *Princess Ida* posters at the beginning of this book were also designed by him for this Princes Theatre season.

For several of the original productions at the Savoy Theatre in the 1880s there were two types of programme available – a tinted paper one for those with cheaper seats and an illustrated card programme for the more expensive parts of the house. All programmes were free of charge.

OPPOSITE **Three attractive programmes designed by Alice Havers for the original productions at the Savoy of** *The Yeomen of the Guard* **(1888),** *Ruddigore* **(1887) and** *The Mikado* **(1885). The** *Yeomen* **programme is interesting in that it contains scenes from an earlier opera, in this case** *Princess Ida.* **(The interior of the** *Mikado* **programme contains scenes from** *H.M.S. Pinafore, The Pirates of Penzance, Patience* **and** *Iolanthe.***)**

ABOVE **An 1883 programme for the original production of** *Iolanthe,* **featuring the fairies and the peers. Several of the** *Patience* **and** *Iolanthe* **programme designs incorporated electric light bulbs to record the fact that the Savoy was the first theatre to be lit throughout by electricity.**

LEFT **A programme for the gala opening night of the Savoy Theatre on October 10, 1881, when the audience first saw an electrically-lit theatre.**

THIS PAGE *The Yeomen of the Guard.*

ABOVE **Jones Hewson (left) as the Lieutenant of the Tower, and Ruth Vincent (right) as Elsie Maynard.**

RIGHT **Rosina Brandram keeps her silent watch and ward as Dame Carruthers, Housekeeper to the Tower.**

OPPOSITE PAGE

ABOVE *A dream of Patience* – **Alice Havers' prizewinning design for a Christmas card competition in 1882. It was used again in January 1885 for the programme of a private performance of Act 2 of *Patience*, which took place at Gilbert's home. The singers were accompanied by François Cellier on the piano and Arthur Sullivan on the harmonium.**

BELOW **An attractive design featuring the costumes of Charles Ricketts and George Sheringham. It was used for the programmes of the 1929 Savoy season.**

In December 1897 Richard D'Oyly Carte presented a new version of Jacques Offenbach's comic opera *The Grand Duchess of Gerolstein*. This was followed by the first revival of *The Gondoliers* and by *The Beauty Stone*, a romantic musical drama by Arthur W. Pinero and J. Comyns Carr with music by Sir Arthur Sullivan. This opera ran for only 50 performances and was replaced by a further run of *The Gondoliers* and by revivals of *Trial by Jury*, *The Sorcerer* and *H.M.S. Pinafore*. Interspersed with these revivals were two new comic operas – *The Lucky Star*, by C. H. Brookfield, Adrian Ross and Aubrey Hopwood with music by Ivan Caryll, and *The Rose of Persia*, or *The Story-teller and the Slave*, by Basil Hood and Sir Arthur Sullivan.

ABOVE LEFT *Ah, how I love the military!*
Florence St. John as the Commander of Hussars in *The Grand Duchess of Gerolstein*.

ABOVE CENTRE Robert Evett as Tapioca, Private Secretary to Baron Tabasco, in *The Lucky Star*. He was a member of the Company from 1892 to 1903.

ABOVE RIGHT *I smoke my hubble-bubble . . .*
Walter Passmore as Hassan, a philanthropist, in *The Rose of Persia*.

OPPOSITE *I'll play for you, stay for you,*
*   Hours on top "A" for you.*
The American coloratura soprano Ellen Beach Yaw as Sultana Zubeydeh (Rose-in-Bloom) in *The Rose of Persia*.

LEFT *See those eyes his eyes enchaining!*
*   Nothing now his heart can stir.*
The Devil has transformed the weaver Simon Limal (Henry Lytton) into a handsome youth who is being seduced by Saida (Pauline Joran) in *The Beauty Stone*.

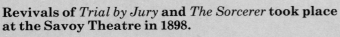

Revivals of *Trial by Jury* and *The Sorcerer* took place at the Savoy Theatre in 1898.

The Sorcerer

ABOVE *The air is charged with amatory numbers.*
Fred Billington, on tour in the British provinces, as Dr Daly, Vicar of Ploverleigh. He assumed the 'Pooh-Bah rôles' in the D'Oyly Carte touring companies for almost 40 years.

ABOVE RIGHT Walter Passmore as John Wellington Wells of J. W. Wells & Co., Family Sorcerers.

Trial by Jury

RIGHT Henry Lytton as the Learned Judge with Isabel Jay as Angelina, the Plaintiff.

The second revival of *H.M.S. Pinafore* took place at the Savoy Theatre from June to November 1899.

ABOVE *Sorry her lot who loves too well,*
Heavy the heart that hopes but vainly . . .
Ruth Vincent as Josephine, Captain Corcoran's daughter, in love with Ralph Rackstraw.

ABOVE RIGHT *It's a song that I have composed for the use of the Royal Navy.*
Sir Joseph Porter, K.C.B. (Walter Passmore) hands his composition to Captain Corcoran (Henry Lytton) and Ralph Rackstraw (Robert Evett).

RIGHT Emmie Owen as Cousin Hebe. She was a member of the Company from 1891 to 1900.

Revivals of *The Pirates of Penzance* and *Patience* took place at the Savoy Theatre in 1900 and 1901. During this period the theatre was closed three times to mark the deaths of Sir Arthur Sullivan (November 22, 1900), Queen Victoria (January 22, 1901) and Richard D'Oyly Carte (April 6, 1901).

OPPOSITE PAGE *The Pirates of Penzance*

ABOVE LEFT Walter Passmore as the Sergeant of Police – a change from his usual lead rôles.

ABOVE RIGHT Isabel Jay as Mabel Stanley.

BELOW LEFT Rosina Brandram as Ruth, a 'piratical maid of all work'.

BELOW RIGHT *Hurrah for the Pirate King!* Jones Hewson sallies forth to seek his prey.

THIS PAGE *Patience*

ABOVE LEFT *Consent at once, or may a nephew's curse –* Bunthorne (Walter Passmore) threatens to curse Grosvenor (Henry Lytton) unless he makes a complete change and becomes a commonplace young man.

ABOVE Jones Hewson, W. H. Leon and Robert Evett as the Colonel, the Major and the Duke in Act 1.

LEFT Isabel Jay in the title rôle.

Miss ISABEL JAY.

Mr ROBERT EVETT

Mr JONES

Miss LOUIE POUNDS

Mr R ROUS.

THE
EMERALD
ISLE

MR. WILLIAM GREET'S
Savoy Theatre Opera Co.

THE
EMERALD
ISLE

Written by
BASIL HOOD
Composed by ARTHUR SULLIVAN
And EDWARD GERMAN

After Richard D'Oyly Carte's death in 1901, the Savoy Theatre was run by his wife Helen, and then by William Greet. There were several new productions including *The Emerald Isle* and *Merrie England*.

OPPOSITE PAGE *The Emerald Isle*

The Emerald Isle, or *The Caves of Carrig Cleena*, was first performed on April 27, 1901, with libretto by Basil Hood and music sketched by Arthur Sullivan and completed by Edward German after Sullivan's death the previous year.

ABOVE The scene in Act 2 in which Professor Bunn of Bath (Walter Passmore) explains how the opera can be brought to a satisfactory conclusion.

BELOW LEFT The composer Edward German (1862–1936).

BELOW RIGHT A poster for *The Emerald Isle*.

THIS PAGE *Merrie England*

Merrie England was first performed on April 2, 1902, with libretto by Basil Hood and music by Edward German.

LEFT *O sleep till I awaken thee,*
And in thy slumber smile!
Rosina Brandram as Queen Elizabeth I.

BELOW LEFT Walter Passmore as Walter Wilkins.

BELOW *Who were the Yeomen – the Yeomen of England?*
Henry Lytton as the Earl of Essex.

The first D'Oyly Carte repertory season took place at the Savoy Theatre from December 1906 to August 1907. The operas presented were *The Yeomen of the Guard*, *The Gondoliers*, *Patience* and *Iolanthe*. *The Mikado* was also to have been performed, but it was banned by the Lord Chamberlain for fear of offending Prince Fushimi of Japan who was visiting England at the time. This action resulted in questions asked in Parliament, a petition to King Edward VII, and substantial financial loss to Helen D'Oyly Carte. W. S. Gilbert was knighted during this season.

OPPOSITE PAGE *The Yeomen of the Guard.*

ABOVE **Tower Green – W. Raphael's impressive set for the 1906 revival of** *The Yeomen of the Guard.*

BELOW *When a wooer goes a-wooing,*
*   Naught is truer than his joy.*
The celebrated quartet from Act 2, with Phoebe Meryll (Jessie Rose), Elsie Maynard (Lilian Coomber), Colonel Fairfax (Pacie Ripple) and a dejected Jack Point (C. H. Workman).

THIS PAGE *The Gondoliers*

ABOVE *At summer day's nooning,*
*   When weary lagooning,*
*   Our mandolins tuning,*
*   We lazily thrum.*
Pacie Ripple and Richard Green as Marco and Giuseppe Palmieri.

LEFT *And vow my complexion derives its perfection*
*   From somebody's soap – which it doesn't.*
Louie René as the Duchess of Plaza-Toro.

THIS PAGE *Patience*

ABOVE **The three aesthetic dragoons in Act 2, as portrayed by Harold Wilde (Duke), Frank Wilson (Colonel) and Richard Andean (Major).**

RIGHT **Clara Dow as Patience, a dairy maid.**

INSET **Louie René as Lady Jane in a pensive mood.**

OPPOSITE PAGE *Iolanthe*

An attractive picture of Clara Dow as Phyllis, an Arcadian shepherdess.

The second D'Oyly Carte repertory season took place at the Savoy Theatre from April 1908 to March 1909. The operas presented were *The Mikado* (whose licence had been restored), *H.M.S. Pinafore*, *Iolanthe*, *The Pirates of Penzance*, *The Gondoliers* and *The Yeomen of the Guard*. Rutland Barrington returned to the Company for this season and played the rôles he had created 20 to 30 years earlier.

The Mikado

ABOVE LEFT *And I am right, and you are right,*
And all is right as right can be!
Pish-Tush (Leicester Tunks), a Noble Lord, informs Nanki-Poo (Strafford Moss) about the Mikado's laws on flirting and of Ko-Ko's elevation from a cheap tailor to the exalted rank of Lord High Executioner. The elaborate set is by A. Terraine.

ABOVE *For they'd none of them be missed –*
they'd none of them be missed.
Charles Herbert Workman as Ko-Ko, the Lord High Executioner of Titipu. He was a member of the Company from 1894 to 1909 and took over the management of the Savoy Theatre from Helen D'Oyly Carte in March 1909.

The Pirates of Penzance

FAR LEFT *With courage rare, and resolution manly,*
For death prepare, unhappy General Stanley.
The Pirate King (Henry Lytton) determines to get his revenge on Major-General Stanley (C. H. Workman).

LEFT A photograph of the Company taken around 1908. Rutland Barrington is in the centre.

The Henry Lytton Years

Henry Lytton as the Duke of Plaza-Toro in *The Gondoliers*

After the London repertory seasons of 1906–07 and 1908–09 the Company continued to tour the British provinces, with Henry Lytton playing all the comedy rôles. He had originally joined the Company in 1884, at the age of 17, and toured with *Princess Ida*. In 1887 he understudied George Grossmith in *Ruddigore* at the Savoy Theatre. He subsequently played a variety of Gilbert and Sullivan rôles – 30 altogether, more than any other Savoyard before or since – and succeeded C. H. Workman in the leading rôles in 1909.

In the following years the company went into decline. There were no London seasons for ten years, Helen D'Oyly Carte died in 1913 (two years after the death of Gilbert) and the First World War began. The Company continued to tour the provinces, but the performances had become fusty and the costumes and scenery were looking dowdy. It was up to Rupert D'Oyly Carte, with his innate sense of the theatre and his shrewd business capacity, to reverse the trend and revitalize the Company.

This he did in grand style. Starting in 1915–18 with a re-dressing of *Iolanthe*, *The Gondoliers* and *Patience*, he was already laying plans for a grand London season once the war was over. To make such a season economically viable, he needed to choose a larger theatre than the Savoy and the Princes Theatre soon became the Company's regular London home.

The 1919–20 Princes Theatre season was a magnificent success. All of the operas were given a new look with fresh scenery and costumes, mainly by W. Bridges-Adams and Percy Anderson respectively. To advertise the season, H. M. Brock and J. Hassall designed an attractive set of posters (see the title pages). Several new principal artists were engaged: in particular, Derek Oldham, Sylvia Cecil, Elsie Griffin and Darrell Fancourt joined the 'resident team' of Henry Lytton, Bertha Lewis, Leo Sheffield, Sydney Granville, Nellie Briercliffe and Frederick Hobbs. The musical director was Geoffrey Toye.

This season caused such a sensation that further London seasons were arranged. *Ruddigore* was added to the repertoire in 1920 with a new overture written by Geoffrey Toye for the 1921–22 London season. *Cox and Box* was revived in 1921. In addition, Rupert D'Oyly Carte formed a second company – the New Opera Company – to satisfy the upsurge in demand in the provinces. This New Company existed from 1919 to 1927 and was to include such names as Martyn Green, Charles Goulding, Leslie Rands and Marjorie Eyre.

To enable Gilbert and Sullivan enthusiasts to enjoy D'Oyly Carte performances in their own homes, Rupert D'Oyly Carte commissioned a series of His Master's Voice recordings. From 1918 to 1925, ten of the operas were issued on 78 r.p.m. discs. These were all Acoustic recordings and gave way to a series of Electric recordings from 1927 onwards. In most of these recordings, George Baker replaced Henry Lytton in the comedy rôles.

The 1926 London season opened with an exciting new production of *The Mikado*, with scenery and costumes designed by Charles Ricketts, one of the foremost English artists of his day. Although highly controversial at first, his designs gradually became popular and continued to be used for many years. The conductor for this season was Dr Malcolm Sargent, thereby beginning a long and happy association with the Company (see page 204).

In October 1929, the Company made a triumphant return to the Savoy Theatre, which had been gutted and largely rebuilt. The season opened with Charles Ricketts' new sets and costumes for *The Gondoliers*. Also receiving a face-lift were *H.M.S. Pinafore*, *The Pirates of Penzance* and *Patience*, with new costumes designed for this season by George Sheringham.

An era ended when Bertha Lewis tragically died as a result of a motoring accident in May 1931. In June 1934 Henry Lytton (now Sir Henry) left the Company after 50 years on the stage. He died in 1936.

Cox and Box, or *The Long-Lost Brothers*, is an adaptation by F. C. Burnand and Arthur Sullivan of *Box and Cox*, a farce by J. Maddison Morton. It was first presented in 1866 and occasionally revived by various D'Oyly Carte companies in the 1890s, but it was not incorporated into the regular repertoire until 1921. Since then it has became a popular curtain-raiser to *H.M.S. Pinafore*, *The Sorcerer* or *The Pirates of Penzance*.

ABOVE **Mr Cox, a journeyman hatter (Leslie Rands), dances with delight on being given the day off.**

ABOVE LEFT *Rataplan, Rataplan, I'm a military man.* **Darrell Fancourt as Sergeant Bouncer, a lodging-house keeper. He was a member of the Company from 1920 to 1953.**

LEFT *I know my notes, I count each bar,*
And I've learnt a tune on the gay guitar.
The 'buttercup serenade', sung by Sydney Granville (Cox) and Leo Darnton (Box).

OPPOSITE **A visit to the Hollywood film studios in February 1929. From left to right: Eleanor Evans, Marjorie Eyre, Bertha Lewis, Ronald Colman (film star), Henry Lytton, Blossom Gelsthorpe, Leslie Rands, Beatrice Elburn and Darrell Fancourt.**

LEFT **The Chorus of Jurymen during the 1919–20 season.**

LEFT BELOW *To marry two at once is Burglaree!* **Counsel for the Plaintiff (Leslie Rands) informs the Court that the Defendant (Robert Wilson) cannot legally marry two wives at the same time.**

BELOW **The Learned Judge (Leo Sheffield) declares his love for Angelina, the Plaintiff (Sylvia Cecil).**

BOTTOM *Tink-a-tank – Tink-a-tank.* **The Defendant (Leo Darnton) accompanies himself on an imaginary guitar, assisted by the Jurymen.**

OPPOSITE **John Wellington Wells (Henry Lytton) summons his noisome hags of night as Alexis (Derek Oldham) comforts Aline (Elsie Griffin).**

LEFT *I am an old fogy, now, am I not, my dear?* **Dr Daly (Leo Sheffield) tells Constance (Nellie Briercliffe) that he intends to remain a bachelor.**

BELOW **Alexis (Charles Goulding) and Aline (Winifred Lawson) sign the marriage contract, watched by Constance, Mrs Partlet, the Notary and Dr Daly.**

BOTTOM **John Wellington Wells (Henry Lytton) yields up his life to Ahrimanes at the end of the opera, watched by Lady Sangazure (Bertha Lewis).**

CENTRE *There is a change in store for you!*
Little Buttercup (Bertha Lewis) warns Captain Corcoran (Leo Sheffield) to be prepared for a change in his situation.

LEFT ABOVE **Henry Lytton as Sir Joseph Porter with Nellie Briercliffe as Cousin Hebe.**

LEFT BELOW *The smartest lad in all the fleet.*
Derek Oldham as Ralph Rackstraw. He was a member of the Company from 1919 to 1922 and for various later seasons.

ABOVE TOP **The Chorus of sisters, cousins and aunts in costumes designed by Percy Anderson for the 1919–20 London season at the Princes Theatre.**

ABOVE **Muriel Dickson as Josephine and Marjorie Eyre as Hebe in costumes designed by George Sheringham for the 1929 season in the refurbished Savoy Theatre.**

CENTRE *With cat-like tread, upon our prey we steal,*
In silence dread our cautious way we feel.
Samuel (Sydney Granville) and the Sergeant of Police (Leo Sheffield) creep stealthily towards each other.

LEFT ABOVE *Ah yes! ah yes! this is exceeding gladness.*
James Hay and Elsie Griffin as Frederic and Mabel in Act 1.

LEFT BELOW *Climbing over rocky mountain,*
Skipping rivulet and fountain,
Passing where the willows quiver . . .
Kate, Edith and Isabel Stanley (Catherine Ferguson, Nellie Briercliffe and Ella Milne) climb down the rocks leading to the bright sea-shore.

ABOVE **A new production of** *The Pirates of Penzance* **was presented at the refurbished Savoy Theatre in 1929. The Act 1 scenery and the costumes for this production were designed by George Sheringham (see also page 118). This is George Sheringham's design for Samuel, the Pirate Lieutenant (Joseph Griffin).**

FAR LEFT ABOVE *For I am blithe and I am gay*
Winifred Lawson as Patience, a dairy maid. She was
a member of the Company from 1922 to 1932.

FAR LEFT BELOW The love-sick maidens in period
costumes designed by Hugo Rumbold in 1918.

CENTRE LEFT ABOVE Lady Jane (Bertha Lewis) and
Reginald Bunthorne (Henry Lytton) agree to
confront Archibald Grosvenor on his home ground.

CENTRE RIGHT ABOVE *If you walk down Piccadilly
with a poppy or a lily in your
mediaeval hand.*
Henry Lytton as the fleshly poet Reginald
Bunthorne.

ABOVE Bertha Lewis as Lady Jane in the costume
designed by George Sheringham for the 1929 Savoy
Theatre season.

LEFT Muriel Dickson as Patience with Marjorie Eyre,
Maisie Baxter and Doreen Denny as the Ladies
Angela, Saphir and Ella.

OPPOSITE *None shall part us from each other,*
One in life and death are we:
All in all to one another –
I to thee and thou to me!
Sydney Granville as Strephon, an Arcadian shepherd, and Helen Gilliland as Phyllis, an Arcadian shepherdess.

LEFT **Leslie Rands as Strephon and (below) Rowena Ronald as Phyllis in costumes designed by George Sheringham for the 1932 Savoy Theatre season.**

BELOW **Lords Mountararat and Tolloller (Darrell Fancourt and Sidney Pointer) endeavour to cheer up the Lord Chancellor (Henry Lytton) who is in love with his ward Phyllis.**

BOTTOM *Bow thy head to Destiny!*
Death thy doom, and thou shall die!
The Queen of the Fairies (Bertha Lewis) pronounces the death sentence on Iolanthe (Catherine Ferguson), watched by the Lord Chancellor (Henry Lytton).

The first London revival of *Princess Ida* took place at the Princes Theatre during the 1919–20 season.

OPPOSITE PAGE

ABOVE *Gently, gently, evidently*
  We are safe so far,
  After scaling fence and paling,
  Here, at last, we are!
Prince Hilarion (Derek Oldham) and his friends Cyril and Florian (Leo Darnton and Sydney Granville) climb into Castle Adamant in search of Princess Ida.

BELOW *Search throughout the panorama*
A group of courtiers in King Hildebrand's palace. The costumes were designed by Percy Anderson (see also page 119) for the 1921–22 London season.

THIS PAGE

ABOVE Lady Blanche (Bertha Lewis) with her daughter Melissa (Nellie Briercliffe).

ABOVE LEFT Princess Ida (Sylvia Cecil) finally accepts the love of Prince Hilarion (James Hay).

LEFT J. M. Gordon, the D'Oyly Carte producer from 1884 to 1930, helps Henry Lytton (King Gama) with a scene from *Princess Ida*.

CENTRE **Ko-Ko (Henry Lytton) insults Pooh-Bah (Leo Sheffield) with a considerable bribe.**

LEFT ABOVE *Ah, shrink not from me!*
Ko-Ko (Henry Lytton) attempts to woo Katisha (Bertha Lewis).

LEFT BELOW *On a cloth untrue, with a twisted cue. . .*
Darrell Fancourt as the Mikado of Japan, a rôle he played more than 3,000 times.

ABOVE TOP *As tough as a bone, with a will of her own*
Bertha Lewis as Katisha in the costume designed by Charles Ricketts for the 1926 London season at the Princes Theatre.

ABOVE **Peep-Bo and Pitti-Sing (Elizabeth Nickell-Lean and Marjorie Eyre) help Yum-Yum (Winifred Lawson) prepare for her wedding day.**

The first London revival of *Ruddigore* took place at the Princess Theatre during the 1921–22 London season, with sets by W. Bridges-Adams (see page 114) and costumes by Percy Anderson.

ABOVE *Cheerily carols the lark*
Over the cot.
Catherine Ferguson as Mad Margaret.

ABOVE LEFT *Oh, my forefathers, wallowers in blood*
Robin Oakapple (Henry Lytton), now Sir Ruthven Murgatroyd, addresses the Ruddigore portraits.

LEFT *Here is a flag that none dare defy, and while this glorious rag floats over Rose Maybud's head, the man does not live who would dare to lay unlicensed hand upon her.*
Dick Dauntless (Derek Oldham) uses a Union Jack to protect Rose Maybud (Elsie Griffin) from Sir Ruthven Murgatroyd's threats.

OPPOSITE PAGE

ABOVE **The Chorus of Bucks and Blades visits the Cornish fishing village of Rederring.**

BELOW *Each Lord of Ruddigore,*
Despite his best endeavour,
Shall do one crime, or more,
Once, every day, for ever!
Bertha Lewis as Dame Hannah describes the Ruddigore curse to the Chorus of bridesmaids. She was a member of the Company from 1906 to 1910 and from 1914 to 1931, when she died as the result of a motoring accident.

The Yeomen of the Guard

ABOVE **Wilfred.** *And thou wilt qualify me as a jester?*
Point. *As a jester among jesters. I will teach thee all my original songs, my self-constructed riddles, my own ingenious paradoxes; nay more, I will reveal to thee the source whence I get them.*
Jack Point (Henry Lytton) agrees to instruct Wilfred Shadbolt (Leo Sheffield) in the art of jestering.

ABOVE RIGHT *What have I done! Oh, woe is me!*
I am his wife, and he is free!
Elsie Maynard (Helen Gilliland) faints into the arms of Colonel Fairfax (Derek Oldham) on learning that the prisoner she has just married has escaped.

FAR RIGHT ABOVE **The Chorus of citizens, dressed in costumes designed by Percy Anderson for the 1919–20 Savoy Theatre season.**

RIGHT **Elsie Maynard (Helen Gilliland) draws a dagger to protect herself from the unruly crowd, after singing** *The Merryman and his Maid.*

FAR RIGHT *I'm a miserable old man, and I've done it – and that's me!*
Sergeant Meryll (Frederick Hobbs) is forced to offer Dame Carruthers (Bertha Lewis) his hand – but not his heart – in return for her silence about his complicity in Colonel Fairfax's escape from the Cold Harbour Tower. Frederick Hobbs sang with the Company from 1914 to 1920, and became its Stage Manager from 1923 to 1927 and Business Manager from 1927 until his death in 1942.

The Gondoliers

ABOVE *At last we have arrived at our destination.*
The Duke of Plaza-Toro (Henry Lytton) arrives in
Venice with the Duchess of Plaza-Toro (Bertha
Lewis) and their daughter Casilda (Sylvia Cecil) to
ascertain the whereabouts of the King of Barataria
to whom Casilda was married in infancy.

LEFT *I stole the Prince, and I brought him here,*
*   And left him gaily prattling*
* With a highly respectable gondolier*
* Who promised the Royal babe to rear. . .*
Leo Sheffield as Don Alhambra del Bolero, the Grand
Inquisitor of Spain, describes how he abducted the
infant son of the King of Barataria and brought him
to Venice. Leo Sheffield was a member of the
Company from 1906 to 1909 and from 1915 to 1930.

OPPOSITE PAGE Hawes Craven (1837–1910), one of
Henry Irving's designers at the Lyceum Theatre,
designed the sets for all of the original productions
from *The Mikado* (1885) to *Utopia Limited* (1893).
Shown here are his lavish and highly-praised sets for
Act 2 of *The Mikado* (Ko-Ko's garden) and Act 2 of
Utopia Limited (The throne room in King
Paramount's palace).

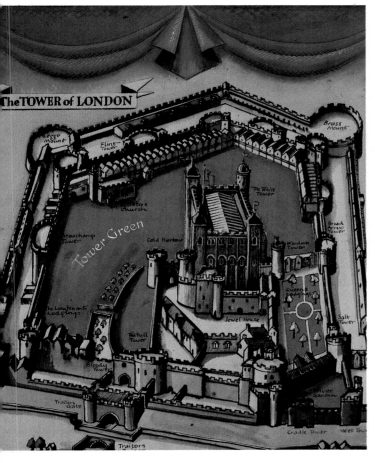

OPPOSITE PAGE **Most of the sets for the 1919 'rebirth' of the operas were designed by W. Bridges-Adams: Act 2 of** *Ruddigore* **– The picture gallery in Ruddigore Castle (above), and Act 2 of** *The Pirates of Penzance* **– A ruined chapel by moonlight (below).**

ABOVE **Charles Ricketts' 1926 set for Act 2 of** *The Mikado* **(Ko-Ko's garden) and his 1929 set for Act 1 of** *The Gondoliers* **(The Piazzetta, Venice).**

LEFT **A pictorial drop curtain for** *The Yeomen of the Guard*, **designed by Peter Goffin (1940).**

WILHELM.
85.

ABOVE A Ladies' Chorus dress for *H.M.S Pinafore*, designed for the original production by Faustin (1847–1914). Faustin also designed the costumes for the original production of *Trial by Jury* in 1875 and the Ladies' Chorus costumes for *The Pirates of Penzance* in 1879.

ABOVE LEFT A dress for Lady Sangazure, designed for the 1884 revival of *The Sorcerer* by C. Wilhelm – a pseudonym for William John Charles Pitcher (1858–1925). This design was, in fact, never used; the handwriting on this sketch, promising a replacement, is that of W. S. Gilbert who himself designed several Savoy costumes. Wilhelm also produced designs for *Iolanthe*, *Princess Ida*, *The Mikado* and *Ruddigore*.

LEFT C. Wilhelm's design for Sir Roderic Murgatroyd in the original production of *Ruddigore* (1887); for this production he also designed all the Ancestors' costumes. His designs were replaced by those of Percy Anderson (1851–1928) for the 1920 revival.

OPPOSITE Wilhelm's design for Nanki-Poo in *The Mikado*. For this production he designed all of the Gentlemen's costumes. His designs were replaced in 1926 by those of Charles Ricketts (1866–1931).

FREDERICK

"PIRATES OF P[...]

George Sh[...]

Peter Goffin/53

TOP **Percy Anderson's designs– King Paramount (1893); The Duke of Plaza-Toro (1917); Princess Ida (1921); Jack Point (1919).**

ABOVE **Charles Ricketts' 1926 designs for Pooh-Bah.**

LEFT **Peter Goffin's designs for Jack Point (1940) and Sir Roderic Murgatroyd (1948).**

FAR LEFT **George Sheringham's 1929 design for Frederic in** *The Pirates of Penzance*.

Costume Designs 1954-1971

LEFT ABOVE **James Wade (1954) – King Hildebrand;
Peter Goffin (1957) – Reginald Bunthorne.**

LEFT BELOW **Osbert Lancaster (1971) – John
Wellington Wells; Bruno Santini (1977) – The Queen
of the Fairies.**

ABOVE **On March 10, 1922 King George V and Queen
Mary attended a performance of** The Gondoliers **at
the Princes Theatre, London, as shown in this
contemporary drawing.** The Gondoliers **has always
been a favourite with the the Royal Family (see
pages 8, 49 and 201).**

ABOVE TOP **Enthusiasts queueing on Friday evening for the last night performance of the 1921–22 London season, to be held the following evening. The operas to be performed on this last night were selected by popular ballot.**

ABOVE **The last night of the 1926 season. Between Rupert D'Oyly Carte and Henry Lytton is Lady Gilbert.**

LEFT **Isidore Godfrey, who joined the 'New Company' in 1925, and was the Company's Musical Director from 1929 to 1968.**

OPPOSITE **The Rebuilding of the Savoy**

ABOVE **In June 1929, Rupert D'Oyly Carte closed the Savoy Theatre for four months. The building was then completely gutted and re-modelled in contemporary style, incorporating all the latest ideas.**

BELOW LEFT **The theatre re-opened on October 21, 1929 with a new production of** *The Gondoliers,* **with sets and costumes designed by Charles Ricketts. This picture shows Ricketts' designs for the Duke and Duchess of Plaza-Toro in Act 2.**

BELOW RIGHT **The interior of the rebuilt and re-modelled Savoy Theatre.**

OLD SAVOYARDS

L.G. (after presentation ceremony): "Well, my dear Lytton, in our time we've both played many parts—for you it's the loving cup—for me it's the bird, look you!"

February 8th, 1934.

Henry Lytton's career with the D'Oyly Carte Opera Company spanned the years 1884–1934. In 1909 he took over the comedy rôles from C. H. Workman and made them his own – especially during the period from 1919 onwards. He was knighted in the 1930 New Year's Honours list. In 1932 he handed over the rôles of Major-General Stanley and Robin Oakapple to his successor Martyn Green. His last London performance was as Ko-Ko at the Savoy Theatre on January 21, 1933, but he continued to tour the provinces for a further 17 months. On February 4, 1934 he celebrated his first 50 years on the stage. He gave his final performance – as Jack Point, his favourite rôle – at the Gaiety Theatre, Dublin, on June 30, 1934. He died on August 15, 1936.

OPPOSITE Sir Henry Lytton with his successor Martyn Green on the day of his farewell performance at the Savoy in January 1933.

INSET A *Daily Express* cartoon (February 8, 1934) of David Lloyd George and Henry Lytton, commemorating Lytton's first 50 years on the stage.

ABOVE *Gentlemen, I'm much touched by this reception.* Sir Henry is toasted by the Company at a reception at the Savoy Theatre following his farewell London performance as Ko-Ko in *The Mikado.*

LEFT Henry Lytton, a keen golfer, enjoys a round of golf with Martyn Green.

BELOW LEFT Lloyd George reads a congratulatory telegram at a luncheon to celebrate Henry Lytton's knighthood in 1930.

125

The Martyn Green Years

Martyn Green as King Gama in *Princess Ida*

Martyn Green succeeded Henry Lytton in 1934. He joined Rupert D'Oyly Carte's 'New Company' in 1922 and toured the smaller provincial theatres, singing in the Chorus and taking some minor principal parts. He soon progressed to five of the comedy rôles and in 1926 was transferred to the main Company as Henry Lytton's understudy, quickly establishing a reputation for his clear singing voice, his sense of timing and his brilliant dancing. In 1932 he assumed the rôles of Robin Oakapple in *Ruddigore* and Major-General Stanley in *The Pirates of Penzance*, and succeeded to the remaining rôles two years later. The other principals at that time included Sydney Granville, Charles Goulding, Darrell Fancourt, Leslie Rands, John Dean, Marjorie Eyre, Muriel Dickson and Dorothy Gill.

In September 1934 the Company sailed to North America for an eight-month visit, beginning with a 15-week season at the Martin Beck Theatre in New York. This was the Company's first visit to New York for over 30 years – a 1927 North American tour visited only Canada and a 1928–29 tour had not included New York. The Martin Beck season was so successful that return visits took place in 1936 (for 18 weeks) and 1939 (for 9½ weeks).

In 1938 a colour film version of *The Mikado* was directed by Victor Schertzinger at the Pinewood Studios, by arrangement with Rupert D'Oyly Carte (see page 142). The cast included several D'Oyly Carte artists, among them Martyn Green as Ko-Ko and Sydney Granville as Pooh-Bah, with the D'Oyly Carte Chorus. The film was adapted and produced by Geoffrey Toye, who was also the Director of Music. The première performance took place at the Leicester Square Theatre on January 12, 1939. Unfortunately, the film proved to be somewhat disappointing and plans to film other Gilbert and Sullivan operas were dropped.

When the Second World War broke out in 1939, the Company was on tour in Bournemouth. All theatres were closed on Government orders and the tour had to be cancelled. The Company was temporarily disbanded, but re-formed as soon as Government restrictions were lifted later in the year. Martyn Green left the Company and joined the Royal Air Force; his place for the duration of the war was taken by Grahame Clifford.

The first war-time season was a four-week visit to the King's Theatre, Edinburgh. The highlight of this season was the first performance, on January 5, 1940, of Peter Goffin's production of *The Yeomen of the Guard* (see page 147). Admired by several critics for being less overbearing than earlier stage sets, his break with tradition was nevertheless very controversial. One critic dismissed the set as 'a Picasso tree and a cement suggestion of the Mersey tunnel'. Goffin's designs eventually became accepted, and this production was the start of a long and successful association between him and the Company.

As the war progressed, the Company continued to present the operas on tour. In some towns Monday night performances had to be discontinued, and in others some of the evening performances gave way to matinées. Air raid warnings during performances were common. In November 1940 the Horsley Street Wardrobe was destroyed in the London blitz (see page 150) and the scenery and costumes for *Ruddigore*, *Princess Ida*, *The Sorcerer* and *H.M.S. Pinafore* were lost. As a consequence, the number of operas on tour was eventually reduced to six. But the touring continued throughout the war without a break, with the Company returning to London once a year to perform in the Savoy, the Princes Theatre or in open-air productions in Brockwell Park and Finsbury Park.

After the war things eventually returned to normal, except for some changes in cast. John Dean, Leslie Rands and Marjorie Eyre left the Company and Martyn Green and Leonard Osborn returned. The other Principals at that time included Ella Halman, Margaret Mitchell, Darrell Fancourt and Richard Walker. They were soon joined by Joan Gillingham, Richard Watson and Thomas Round. Richard Collet, General Manager since 1919, died in 1946.

At the end of 1947 the Company made its first postwar visit to the United States, performing in New York and Boston. During this tour it became clear that the word 'nigger', which appeared in three places in the operas, was considered offensive and Rupert D'Oyly Carte commissioned A. P. Herbert to make the necessary changes. The United States tour was so successful that the Company found itself increasingly making visits to North America. Such tours were financially advantageous and enabled the Company and the British audiences periodically to have a break from each other.

In November 1948 a new production of *Ruddigore* was presented in Newcastle with a new Act 2 set and new costumes designed by Peter Goffin. Shortly before this, in the midst of the preparations for this production, Rupert D'Oyly Carte died. He was succeeded by his daughter Bridget, who continued to run the Company for the next 33 years.

The Martyn Green years concluded with the Festival of Britain season which took place at the Savoy Theatre from May 7 to August 4, 1951. At the end of this season Martyn Green left the Company, eventually to settle permanently in New York where he appeared in various productions of the operas on stage and television, as well as taking part in many plays. He had a serious accident in a New York lift which necessitated the immediate amputation of a leg, but he courageously continued to perform on the stage and television until his death in 1975.

Cox and Box continued to provide a curtain-raiser for *H.M.S. Pinafore* and *The Sorcerer* during the Martyn Green years, although *The Sorcerer* was performed only rarely. It was dropped from the repertoire during the war years when the scenery and costumes of these two operas were destroyed, but was reinstated in 1947.

ABOVE *None but I on the cliff so high,*
And all save the sea was bare and dry,
And I took one look on the wave below,
And I raised my hands in an agony throe,
And I stood on the edge of the rock so steep,
And I gazed like a maniac on the deep.
Mr Box (John Dean) graphically describes to Mr Cox (George Cammidge) how he faked an imaginary suicide to escape the attentions of Penelope Ann.

LEFT Martyn Green as Mr Cox is amazed to discover a rasher of bacon that his room-mate Mr Box has left cooking on the gridiron. Martyn Green first played this rôle in 1924 and continued to play it until 1935.

OPPOSITE Members of the Company en route to New York for a North American tour. Among those pictured here are Martyn Green, Darrell Fancourt, Leslie Rands, John Dean, Sydney Granville, Richard Walker and Marjorie Eyre.

129

THIS PAGE *The Sorcerer*

The Sorcerer was performed only rarely during the Martyn Green years. It was presented in London in 1938 and 1939, but was dropped from the repertoire when the scenery and costumes were destroyed in the war. It was not performed again by the Company until 1971.

ABOVE *Give me the love that loves for love alone –*
I love that love – I love it only!
John Dean and Ann Drummond-Grant as Alexis the brave and the lovely Aline.

LEFT *Our penny Curse – one of the cheapest things*
in the trade – is considered infallible.
Martyn Green as John Wellington Wells, the 'dealer in magic and spells'.

OPPOSITE PAGE *Trial by Jury*

MAIN PICTURE **Richard Walker as the Usher confers with Sydney Granville as the Learned Judge.**

INSET *Yet of beauty I'm a judge*
Leslie Rands as the Learned Judge. He was a member of the Company from 1925 to 1947.

H.M.S. Pinafore **was not performed by the Company from 1940 to 1947 as the scenery and costumes had been destroyed during the London blitz (see page 150).**

ABOVE LEFT *Oh, bitter is my cup!*
However could I do it?
I mixed those children up,
And not a creature knew it!

Evelyn Gardiner as Little Buttercup, a Portsmouth bumboat woman, admits that she interchanged Ralph Rackstraw and Captain Corcoran in infancy.

ABOVE RIGHT **Richard Walker as Bill Bobstay, the boatswain's mate. He was a member of the Company for over 20 years and inherited the 'Pooh-Bah rôles' from Sydney Granville.**

LEFT *I am the monarch of the sea,*
The ruler of the Queen's Navee,
Whose praise Great Britain loudly chants.

Martyn Green as Sir Joseph Porter, K.C.B., First Lord of the Admiralty.

OPPOSITE *Sing hey, the cat-o'-nine-tails and the tar.*
The merry cat-o'-nine tails and the tar.

Dick Deadeye (Darrell Fancourt) has just warned Captain Corcoran (Leslie Rands) of Ralph Rackstraw's imminent elopement with Josephine. The Captain determines to take revenge on Ralph.

133

FAR LEFT *We object to Major-Generals as fathers-in-law. But we waive that point. We do not press it. We look over it.*

The Pirate King (Darrell Fancourt) puts Major-General Stanley (Martyn Green) in his place when the latter objects to the pirates' intention to wed his bevy of beautiful daughters.

LEFT *Tormented with the anguish dread*
Of falsehood unatoned,
I lay upon my sleepless bed,
And tossed and turned and groaned.

Disturbed by the 'cat-like tread' of the pirates, and tormented by his falsehood that he was an orphan, the Major-General (Martyn Green) finds himself unable to sleep.

ABOVE *Go to death, and go to slaughter;*
Die, and every Cornish daughter
With her tears your grave shall water.
Go, ye heroes, go and die!

Muriel Dickson as Mabel and Sydney Granville as the Sergeant of Police, as the policemen brave themselves to face the pirates.

ABOVE LEFT *Let the merry cymbals sound*
Lady Angela and Lady Saphir (Marjorie Eyre and Kathleen Naylor) serenade a miserable Bunthorne (Martyn Green) in the Finale of Act 1.

ABOVE *I, who alone am faithful to him, shall reap my reward. But do not dally too long, Reginald, for my charms are ripe, Reginald, and already they are decaying. Better secure me ere I have gone too far.*
Ella Halman as Lady Jane at the beginning of Act 2.

ABOVE RIGHT **Martyn Green as Reginald Bunthorne admires himself in Archibald Grosvenor's mirror.**

FAR LEFT *Cling passionately to one another and think of faint lilies.*
At Bunthorne's request, Colonel Calverley, the Duke of Dunstable and Major Murgatroyd (Darrell Fancourt, John Dean and William Sumner) prepare themselves to understand his poem *Oh, Hollow! Hollow! Hollow!*.

LEFT **Dorothy Gill as Lady Jane and Marjorie Eyre as Lady Angela.**

RIGHT *Great Heavens, what is there to adulate in me?*
John Dean as Lieut. the Duke of Dunstable. He was a member of the Company from 1926 to 1946.

LEFT ABOVE *When tempests wreck thy bark,*
And all is drear and dark,
If thou shouldst need an Ark,
I'll give thee one!
Marjorie Eyre as Iolanthe. She was a member of the Company from 1924 to 1946, playing the soprano rôles in the 'New Company' before changing to the soubrette rôles. She was married to Leslie Rands.

LEFT BELOW *The Law is the true embodiment*
Of everything that's excellent.
It has no kind of fault or flaw,
And I, my Lords, embody the Law.
The Lord Chancellor (Martyn Green) introduces himself in his opening song.

CENTRE *Spurn not the nobly born*
With love affected,
Nor treat with virtuous scorn
The well-connected.
Herbert Garry as Earl Tolloller tries to persuade Phyllis that high rank involves no shame and that the peerage is not destitute of virtue.

ABOVE *Tripping hither, tripping thither,*
Nobody knows why or whither;
We must dance and we must sing
Round about our fairy ring!
Margery Abbott, Ivy Sanders and Kathleen Naylor as the dainty little fairies Celia, Leila and Fleta as they sing and dance at the beginning of the opera.

139

ABOVE **The Courtyard of Castle Adamant – the set for Act 3, designed by W. Bridges-Adams for use during the North American tour of 1936–37. It was destroyed during the London blitz.**

LEFT *And I'm a peppery kind of King*
Who's indisposed for parleying
To fit the wit of a bit of a chit,
And that's the long and the short of it!
Richard Watson as the peppery King Hildebrand arrives at Castle Adamant with his army of soldiers.

OPPOSITE *To-morrow morn fair Ida we'll engage;*
But we will use no force her love to gain,
Nature has armed us for the war we wage!
Charles Goulding as Prince Hilarion in his Act 1 costume. He was a member of the Company from 1919 to 1936, and played all of the leading tenor rôles.

INSET *Mighty maiden with a mission –*
Paragon of common sense;
Running fount of erudition –
Miracle of eloquence!
Ann Drummond-Grant as Princess Ida. She was a member of the Company from 1932 to 1939 and 1950 to 1959, quickly progressing to the leading soprano rôles. In later years her voice deepened and she assumed all the contralto rôles. She was married to the conductor Isidore Godfrey.

141

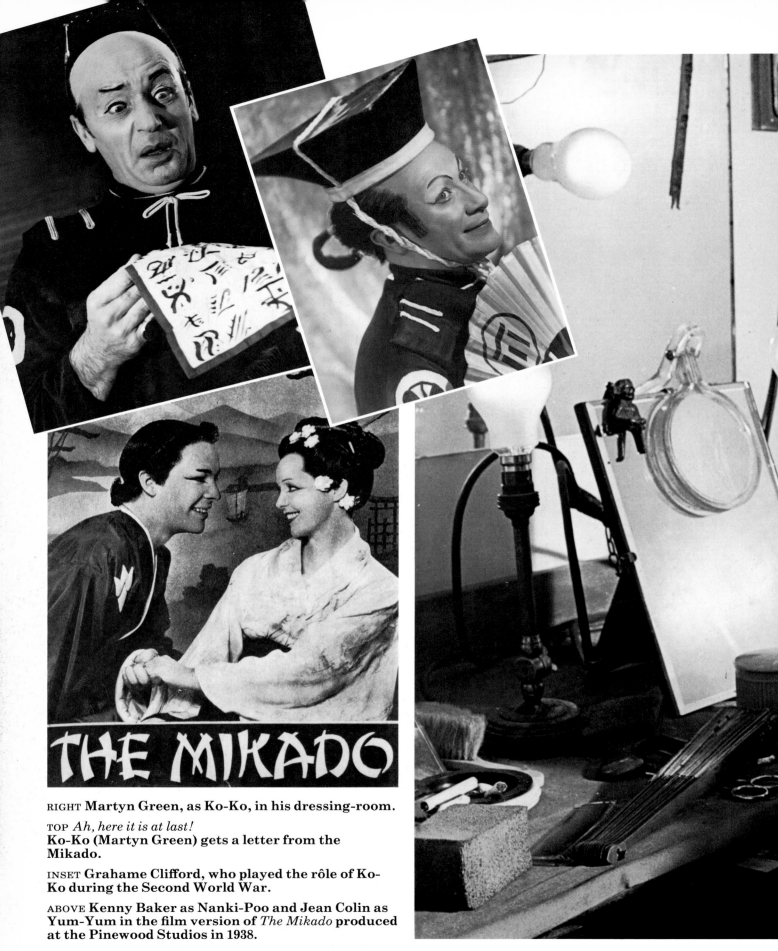

THE MIKADO

RIGHT **Martyn Green, as Ko-Ko, in his dressing-room.**

TOP *Ah, here it is at last!*
Ko-Ko (Martyn Green) gets a letter from the Mikado.

INSET **Grahame Clifford, who played the rôle of Ko-Ko during the Second World War.**

ABOVE **Kenny Baker as Nanki-Poo and Jean Colin as Yum-Yum in the film version of** *The Mikado* **produced at the Pinewood Studios in 1938.**

142

A new production of *Ruddigore* was presented in Newcastle on November 1, 1948. This was the first production of this opera by the Company since the sets and costumes were destroyed during the London blitz. The Act 2 set and the costumes for this new production were by Peter Goffin (1906–1974).

OPPOSITE PAGE

ABOVE Peter Goffin with the set that he designed in 1957 for Act 1.

BELOW LEFT *And painful though that duty be,*
To shirk the task were fiddle-de-dee!
Sir Despard Murgatroyd (Richard Watson) and Dick Dauntless (Leonard Osborn) agree to expose Robin Oakapple as a bad Baronet of Ruddigore.

BELOW RIGHT *Curdle the heart-blood in his arteries, and freeze the very marrow in his bones.*
Old Adam Goodheart (Radley Flynn) and Robin Oakapple (Martyn Green) consider how to deal with Dick Dauntless.

THIS PAGE

ABOVE The Picture Gallery in Ruddigore Castle – Peter Goffin's stage set for Act 2.

LEFT Ella Halman as Dame Hannah, Rose Maybud's aunt. She was a member of the Company from 1937 to 1951, and inherited all the contralto rôles from Evelyn Gardiner at the beginning of the war.

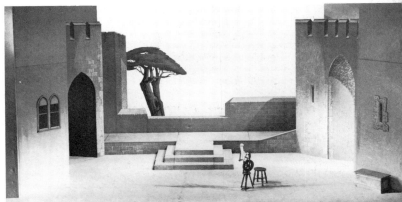

The Yeomen of the Guard

FAR LEFT *It's a song of a merryman, moping mum,*
Whose soul was sad, and whose glance was glum,
Who sipped no sup, and who craved no crumb,
As he sighed for the love of a ladye!
Martyn Green as Jack Point with Muriel Dickson as Elsie Maynard.

CENTRE *Forbear, my friends, and spare me this ovation,*
I have small claim to such consideration.
Colonel Fairfax (John Dean), masquerading as Leonard Meryll, meets his fellow Yeomen.

CENTRE LEFT **Ann Drummond-Grant as Elsie Maynard.**

LEFT *'Tis but a little word – "heigho!"*
Marjorie Eyre as Phoebe Meryll.

ABOVE **On January 5, 1940 a new production of** *The Yeomen of the Guard* **was presented in Edinburgh. The scenery and costumes were designed by Peter Goffin (see pages 115 and 118). His controversial stage set was designed to focus attention on the action of the opera and not to detract from it. Jack Point played by Grahame Clifford who assumed the comedy rôles during the war.**

147

ABOVE *Come, let's away – our island crown awaits me.*
Marco and Giuseppe (John Dudley and Leslie Rands) prepare to leave for the balmy island of Barataria at the end of Act 1.

ABOVE LEFT *This polite attention touches*
Heart of Duke and heart of Duchess
Martyn Green and Evelyn Gardiner as the Duke and Duchess of Plaza-Toro make their arrival at the Court of Barataria.

LEFT *I am a courtier grave and serious*
Who is about to kiss your hand:
Try to combine a pose imperious
With a demeanour nobly bland.
Graham Clifford as the Duke of Plaza-Toro. Gilbert originally intended this song as a minuet, but later changed his mind and wrote a gavotte.

OPPOSITE PAGE

LEFT *And his Grace's private drum*
Herbert Garry as Luiz, the 'musical young man who is such a past-master of that delicately modulated instrument'.

ABOVE RIGHT *Then hail, O King of a Golden Land,*
And the high-born bride who claims his hand!
Luiz and Casilda (John Dean and Eileen Moody) assume the throne of Barataria at the end of the opera.

BELOW RIGHT Tessa and Gianetta (Marjorie Eyre and Muriel Dickson) console each other as the gondoliers depart for Barataria. Muriel Dickson was a member of the Company from 1928 to 1935.

LEFT **On November 17, 1940 the Horsley Street wardrobe and scene store in south-east London were destroyed by enemy action during the London blitz. The result of this was the loss of the scenery and costumes of four of the operas – *The Sorcerer*, *H.M.S. Pinafore*, *Princess Ida* and *Ruddigore*. The first of these operas to be reinstated into the Company's repertoire was *H.M.S. Pinafore* in 1947, followed by *Ruddigore* in 1948, *Princess Ida* in 1954 and finally *The Sorcerer* in 1971.**

ABOVE **An informal photograph of the three little maids from school (Joyce Wright, Joan Gillingham and Margaret Mitchell) participating in the Japanese tea ceremony at the stage door canteen at Sadler's Wells Theatre, London, during a rehearsal of *The Mikado*.**

INSET **Over the years the D'Oyly Carte Company has made many recordings, covering all of the operas except *Thespis* (most of the music of which is lost). Before the war these were His Master's Voice recordings under the direction of Rupert D'Oyly Carte. Only one of them (*The Mikado*, recorded in 1936) featured Martyn Green. After the war, Bridget D'Oyly Carte initiated a set of Decca recordings, starting with *Trial by Jury* in 1949 and continuing with eight recordings featuring Martyn Green. The record sleeves shown above are *The Mikado* (1950), *Trial by Jury* (1949) and *Ruddigore* (1950). Later record sleeves are shown on pages 155 and 203.**

The Peter Pratt Years

Peter Pratt as Bunthorne in *Patience*

When the Company reassembled after the Festival of Britain season there were many changes in the cast. Martyn Green's place in the comedy rôles was taken by his understudy Peter Pratt, who had joined the Company in 1945 as a member of the Chorus. Darrell Fancourt, Leonard Osborn, Neville Griffiths and Alan Styler remained, but Richard Watson, Margaret Mitchell and Jean Gillingham were replaced by Fisher Morgan, Shirley Hall and Joyce Wright respectively. The husband-and-wife team of Radley Flynn and Ella Halman was succeeded by Sydney Allen and Ann Drummond-Grant; the latter had played the principal soprano rôles in the 1930s, but her voice had deepened and she now assumed the contralto rôles. Her husband, Isidore Godfrey, continued as Director of Music and Frederic Lloyd took over as General Manager. It was a difficult time for the Company, but the new blood was invigorating and resulted in a general improvement in standards.

In the Queen's Birthday Honours list for 1953, Darrell Fancourt received the O.B.E. He had been unwell with eye trouble for some time and reluctantly decided to retire at the end of the Coronation Season at Sadler's Wells Theatre. But he was too ill to complete the season and he died in August 1953, only six weeks after his last performance. His widow, Eleanor Evans, retired as Director of Productions and was replaced by Robert Gibson, a former stage manager at Radio City Music Hall. Darrell Fancourt's place in the Company was taken by Donald Adams.

In 1949 Bridget D'Oyly Carte had initiated a series of Decca recordings of the operas and eight of them were recorded with Martyn Green. This series was continued during the Peter Pratt years with recordings of *Patience* (1952), *The Sorcerer* (1953), *Princess Ida* (1955), *The Pirates of Penzance* (1958) and *The Mikado* (1959).

A Technicolor film biography of the Gilbert and Sullivan partnership, *The Story of Gilbert and Sullivan*, was produced in 1953 at the Shepperton Studios by Frank Launder and Sidney Gilliat (see page 173). Robert Morley and Maurice Evans starred as W. S. Gilbert and Arthur Sullivan, with Peter Finch and Eileen Herlie as Richard and Helen D'Oyly Carte. The film was officially sanctioned by the D'Oyly Carte Company and featured a number of former Savoyards, including Martyn Green (as George Grossmith), Thomas Round, Webster Booth and Joan Gillingham. The music was conducted by Sir Malcolm Sargent.

During the 1950s there were several new productions. In December 1952 new stage sets for *The Mikado* were designed by Peter Goffin to replace the Ricketts' designs which had done good service since 1926. In 1954 the fairies' costumes in *Iolanthe* were redesigned by Pat Freeborn. In January 1957 a new production of *Patience* was presented at the Princes Theatre, London, with sets and costumes designed by Peter Goffin (see page 161). But the most important new production was that of *Princess Ida* in 1954. This exciting production was presented at the Savoy Theatre with Robert Gibson as producer and with costumes and stage sets designed by James Wade to give 'a fantastic dream-like quality' (see page 170). This was the first production of *Princess Ida* since the sets and costumes were destroyed during the London blitz.

In 1955–56 the Company celebrated the 75th anniversary of its first visit to the United States by embarking on a seven-month tour of North America. This visit started with a month's stay at the Central City Opera House in the Colorado Rockies and included a colourful ceremony (see page 175) at which Bruce Worsley, the Company's Business Manager, and Frederic Lloyd, its General Manager, were elected Honorary Indian Chiefs of the Sioux tribe.

The expense of touring with several different operas is enormous, especially when the sets are as complicated as those of *Princess Ida*, for example. To reduce the costs of touring Peter Goffin conceived the idea of a 'unit set', consisting of a basic structure fixed to the sides of the stage to which painted panels for each opera can be attached. This simple but effective idea had the desired result – the number of vans needed to carry the scenery was reduced from 20 to nine. The unit set was introduced in October 1957 and the sets of all the operas were adapted to fit it. When Peter Goffin redesigned *The Gondoliers* in 1958 he planned it for the unit set from the beginning.

The Winter season of 1958–59 at the Princes Theatre, London, was a memorable one. Thomas Round had rejoined the Company and Kenneth Sandford, Jeffrey Skitch and Jennifer Toye were recent recruits. On the last night the Company presented a 'pot-pourri' consisting of Act 2 of *Iolanthe*, Act 2 of *The Gondoliers*, an overture and an extraordinary performance of *Trial by Jury* (see page 157) in which the entire cast was dressed in costumes from the other operas. These last-night revelries were to become a regular feature of the London seasons from 1959 onwards and were a good opportunity to see the Company 'let its hair down'.

This last night at the Princes Theatre was to be the last London performance of Ann Drummond-Grant and Peter Pratt. Ann Drummond-Grant became seriously ill in the spring of 1959 and died in September. Peter Pratt decided that he wished to make a change and left the Company in May after playing the comedy rôles for eight years. His diverse activities since then have included several Gilbert and Sullivan radio programmes.

ABOVE *Cox and Box* Eric Thornton as Sergeant Bouncer greets Alan Styler as Mr Cox at the beginning of the opera.

LEFT *Cox and Box* Frederick Sinden as Box, George Cook as Bouncer and John Reed as Cox celebrate the reunion of the long-lost brothers.

INSET *The Sorcerer* After the destruction of the scenery and costumes during the war, *The Sorcerer* was not performed again until 1971. It was, however, recorded in 1953 with Peter Pratt in the title rôle.

OPPOSITE **Fisher Morgan, Joyce Wright, Peter Pratt and Donald Adams relax during the 1955–56 tour of North America.**

ABOVE **John Reed (left) and Fisher Morgan (right) in two portrayals of the Learned Judge.**

FAR LEFT *Now, Jurymen, hear my advice.*
Ivor Evans as the Usher addresses the members of the Jury.

INSET **Four members of the Chorus – James Marsland, Alice Hynd, Jack Habbick and May Sanderson.**

LEFT **An extraordinary performance of** *Trial by Jury* **on the last night of the 1958–59 London season, in which the cast wore costumes from the other operas.**

157

THIS PAGE *H.M.S. Pinafore*

ABOVE *I say – it's a beast of a name, ain't it?*
Donald Adams as Dick Deadeye. He was a member of the Company from 1951 to 1969 and took over the 'Mikado rôles' from Darrell Fancourt in 1953.

ABOVE RIGHT *Fair moon, to thee I sing*
Bright regent of the heavens . . .
Eric Thornton as Captain Corcoran serenades the heavens at the beginning of Act 2.

RIGHT **Sir Joseph Porter (Peter Pratt) reluctantly accepts the hand of Cousin Hebe (Joyce Wright) at the end of Act 2.**

OPPOSITE PAGE *The Pirates of Penzance*

ABOVE *You are the victim of this clumsy arrangement having been born in leap-year, on the twenty-ninth of February*
Neville Griffiths as Frederic cuts a birthday cake on February 29, 1956, watched by Muriel Harding (Mabel) and members of the Chorus.

BELOW LEFT **Thomas Round as Frederic, the Pirate Apprentice. He was a member of the Company from 1946 to 1949 and from 1958 to 1964.**

BELOW RIGHT *And it is – it is a glorious thing*
To be a Major-General!
Peter Pratt as Major-General Stanley.

ABOVE **The Officers of Dragoon Guards relax in their dressing room during Act 2.**

LEFT *I cannot tell what this love may be
That cometh to all but not to me.*
Muriel Harding as Patience, a dairy maid.

BELOW RIGHT **Peter Pratt as Reginald Bunthorne, crowned with roses and hung about with garlands.**

THIS PAGE **A new production of *Patience* was presented at the Princes Theatre, London, in January 1957. The scenery and costumes were designed by Peter Goffin (see also page 120).**

LEFT *Silvered is the raven hair*
Lady Jane (Ann Drummond-Grant) accompanies herself on a 'cello as she rues her advancing age.

ABOVE *You hold yourself like this!*
Major Murgatroyd (John Reed), Lieut. the Duke of Dunstable (Leonard Osborn) and Colonel Calverley (Donald Adams) realize that the only way of making an impression on the love-sick maidens is to become as aesthetic as they are.

ABOVE *Blue blood! Blue blood!*
Leonard Osborn as Earl Tolloller. He was a member of the Company for 15 years and later became its Production Director.

ABOVE RIGHT *The constitutional guardian I*
Of pretty young Wards in Chancery,
All very agreeable girls – and none
Are over the age of twenty-one.
Peter Pratt in the rôle of the highly susceptible Lord Chancellor.

RIGHT **Ann Drummond-Grant as the Queen of the Fairies. In the 1930s she played the soprano rôles of Phyllis and Celia, and later sang the title rôle in the 1952 Decca recording.**

OPPOSITE PAGE

ABOVE LEFT **Fisher Morgan as Private Willis of the 1st Grenadier Guards.**

ABOVE RIGHT **Joyce Wright as Iolanthe. She was a member of the Company from 1947 to 1962.**

BELOW *Tantantara! Tzing! Boom!*
At the first performance of *Iolanthe* in 1882 the entry of the Chorus of Peers was augmented by the band of the Grenadier Guards. This picture shows the 75th anniversary performance at Streatham Hill on November 25, 1957 when the idea was repeated.

The Mikado

ABOVE *I am, in point of fact, a particularly haughty and exclusive person of pre-Adamite ancestral descent. You will understand this when I tell you that I can trace my ancestry back to a protoplasmal primordial atomic globule.*
Arthur Richards as Pooh-Bah, the Lord High Everything Else in the town of Titipu.

ABOVE RIGHT *A wandering minstrel I –*
A thing of shreds and patches,
Of ballads, songs and snatches,
And dreamy lullaby!
Thomas Round as Nanki-Poo, the son of the Mikado. He is visiting Titipu in search of Yum-Yum whom he loves so dearly.

RIGHT *To sit in solemn silence in a dull, dark dock,*
In a pestilential prison, with a life-long lock.
Ko-Ko (Peter Pratt), the Lord High Executioner, has just received a letter from the Mikado requiring him to carry out an execution within one month.

FAR RIGHT *My object all sublime*
I shall achieve in time –
To let the punishment fit the crime –
The punishment fit the crime.
Donald Adams as his Majesty, the Mikado of Japan.

Ruddigore

THIS PAGE *Ruddigore*

RIGHT *I've given up all my wild proceedings*
Despard Murgatroyd (Kenneth Sandford) is now leading a pure and blameless life after his ten years of evil misdeeds.

BELOW *Hey, but he's timid as a youth can be!*
Peter Pratt as Robin Oakapple in Act 1.

BELOW RIGHT *This hallowed volume, composed, if I may believe the title page, by no less an authority than the wife of a Lord Mayor, has been, through life, my guide and monitor.*
Jean Barrington as Rose Maybud with her book of etiquette.

OPPOSITE PAGE *The Yeomen of the Guard*

ABOVE LEFT *And a lively one I'll be,*
Wag-a-wagging, never flagging!
Kenneth Sandford as Wilfred Shadbolt, Head Jailer and Assistant Tormentor.

ABOVE RIGHT Alan Styler as Sir Richard Cholmondeley, Lieutenant of the Tower. He was a member of the Company from 1947 to 1968.

BELOW *A man who would woo a fair maid*
Should 'prentice himself to the trade
The trio from Act 2 in which Colonel Fairfax (Leonard Osborn), Phoebe Meryll (Joyce Wright) and Elsie Maynard (Muriel Harding) instruct Jack Point (Peter Pratt) in the art of wooing.

In 1957–58 a new production of *The Gondoliers* was presented at the Princes Theatre, London. This was the first new production of this opera since Charles Ricketts' version in 1929 and was well received. The scenery and costumes were designed by Peter Goffin. This was the first production designed specifically to fit the 'unit set' – an ingenious device designed for easier and cheaper touring (see page 154).

LEFT ABOVE Peter Goffin's set for Act 2 – a Pavilion in the Court of Barataria.

LEFT CENTRE *Bridegroom and bride!*
Giuseppe and Marco (Alan Styler and Thomas Round) arrive with their brides Tessa and Gianetta (Joyce Wright and Jean Hindmarsh) in a gondola propelled by gondolier Alan Barrett.

LEFT BELOW *Of that there is no manner of doubt –*
No probable, possible shadow of doubt –
No possible doubt whatever.
Kenneth Sandford as Don Alhambra del Bolero, the Grand Inquisitor of Spain. He joined the Company in 1957 and played the 'Pooh-Bah rôles' until its demise in 1982.

CENTRE *From the sunny Spanish shore,*
The Duke of Plaza-Tor' –
And his Grace's Duchess true –
Peter Pratt and Ann Drummond-Grant as the Duke and Duchess of Plaza-Toro arriving in Venice in Act 1.

ABOVE Jennifer Toye as Casilda in Act 2.

Princess Ida

On September 27, 1954 a new production of *Princess Ida* was presented at the Savoy Theatre. The scenery and costumes were designed by James Wade (see page 120), and the producer was Robert Gibson.

ABOVE TOP The Gardens of Castle Adamant – James Wade's fantastic dream-like setting for Act 2. It was decided that a literal interpretation of this opera was inappropriate for the 1950s.

ABOVE *Oh, Cyril, how I dread this interview.*
King Hildebrand (Fisher Morgan) admits to Cyril (Leonard Osborn) his nervousness about meeting the crusty King Gama.

RIGHT Two portrayals of the title rôle in the 1950s. Jean Hindmarsh (centre) invokes Minerva, the goddess of wisdom, in Act 2, while Victoria Sladen (far right) prepares to face King Hildebrand's soldiers in Act 3 after all her women students have deserted her.

THIS PAGE *Princess Ida*

ABOVE LEFT **Cynthia Morey as Lady Psyche in Act 3, preparing to defend Castle Adamant.**

ABOVE *Sing hoity-toity! Sorry for some!*
Beryl Dixon as Melissa, Lady Blanche's daughter.

LEFT *Today we meet, my baby bride and I –*
  But ah, my hopes are balanced by my fears!
John Fryatt as Hilarion looks forward to meeting Princess Ida to whom he was betrothed in infancy.

OPPOSITE PAGE *The Story of Gilbert and Sullivan*
A Technicolor film biography of the Gilbert and Sullivan partnership was produced at the Shepperton Studios in 1953. It featured a number of D'Oyly Carte artists, including Martyn Green and Thomas Round.

ABOVE **The 'carpet quarrel' scene, in which W. S. Gilbert (Robert Morley) demands an explanation from Richard D'Oyly Carte (Peter Finch) concerning the cost of new carpets for the front of the Savoy Theatre (see page 52). Arthur Sullivan (Maurice Evans) and Helen D'Oyly Carte (Eileen Herlie) look on.**

BELOW LEFT **Thomas Round as the Defendant and Yvonne Marsh as the Plaintiff in *Trial by Jury*.**

BELOW RIGHT **Arthur Sullivan conducts a rehearsal of *The Mikado*.**

OPPOSITE PAGE **Backstage**

ABOVE LEFT **Harry Haste, the Company's Master Carpenter from 1919 to 1962.**

ABOVE RIGHT *Paint the pretty face – Dye the coral lip.*

BELOW LEFT **Clarice Blain, the Wardrobe Mistress, irons Josephine's dress before** *H.M.S. Pinafore.*

BELOW RIGHT **H.M.S. Pinafore receives a new coat of paint at the Harker Bros. Scenic Studios.**

THIS PAGE **Central City, Colorado**

To celebrate the 75th anniversary of its first visit to the United States, the Company embarked on a seven-month extended tour of North America. At the beginning of this tour, in July 1955, the Company spent four enjoyable weeks in the Colorado Rockies at the opera house in Central City. During this visit a ceremony took place in which Bruce Worsley and Frederic Lloyd (the Company's Business Manager and General Manager) were elected Honorary Indian Chiefs of the Sioux tribe.

LEFT **The initiation of Bruce Worsley as Chief Eagle Pipe of the Sioux tribe. Chief Charlie Red Cloud smokes the pipe of peace, watched by Chief Sitting Hawk and Chief Andrew Fool's Crow.**

ABOVE **Members of the Company pose with Indians from the Sioux tribe in Central City.**

The John Reed Years

John Reed as Sir Joseph Porter in *H.M.S. Pinafore*

John Reed joined the Company in November 1951 as a member of the Chorus and understudy to Peter Pratt. He grew up in Darlington and was well known in north-east England as a talented actor, singer and dancer. His transition to the principal rôles in 1959 was painless and he was soon greeted with enthusiasm by the Gilbert and Sullivan public. During his 20 years in these rôles he witnessed many changes in cast; these are too numerous to be listed here, but are chronicled on the following pages.

At the end of 1961 the Company's monopoly on the operas disappeared with the expiry of the copyright. Some people feared that this might harm the Company, but this proved not to be the case. Although Gilbert and Sullivan enthusiasts were now able to see several styles of performance, the D'Oyly Carte continued to be as popular as ever. It was around this time that Bridget D'Oyly Carte formed the D'Oyly Carte Opera Trust, Ltd.

The Company continued to issue recordings and all of the operas were re-recorded with John Reed in the principal rôles. *Utopia Limited* and *The Grand Duke* were issued for the first time, as were Sullivan's *Imperial March, Marmion Overture, The Zoo* and some incidental music for *Macbeth* and *Henry VIII*. Guest artists included Owen Brannigan and Elizabeth Harwood, and Sir Malcolm Sargent was guest conductor for *The Yeomen of the Guard* and *Princess Ida*.

The Company was also increasingly involved with film and television. A new film of *The Mikado* was made in 1967 and television broadcasts of *Patience* (1965) and *H.M.S. Pinafore* (1973) were made. It also provided the soundtrack for a Halas and Batchelor cartoon film of *Ruddigore*.

Several of the operas were given a new look during the John Reed years. Peter Goffin redesigned *H.M.S Pinafore* in 1961 and George Foa redirected *The Gondoliers* in 1962 with scenery by Stephen Bundy. Anthony Besch redirected *The Mikado* in 1964 with sets by Disley Jones, and also produced a controversial new version of *The Gondoliers* with sets by John Stoddart and costumes by Luciana

Arrighi (see page 200). On March 29, 1971 a splendid new production of *The Sorcerer* was presented at the Opera House, Manchester, produced by Michael Heyland and with sets and costumes by Osbert Lancaster, C.B.E. (see page 182). This was the first production of *The Sorcerer* since the sets and costumes were destroyed during the London blitz. During the Centenary Season (see below) *Utopia Limited* was presented for the first time since its original run in 1893–94, with sets by Peter Rice. Finally, on July 12, 1977 an attractive new production of *Iolanthe* was presented at Sadler's Wells, with sets and costumes by Bruno Santini (see page 190).

For many people, the highlight of the John Reed years was the Centenary Season in 1975. This two-week season at the Savoy Theatre started with a Gala Evening on March 25, the 100th anniversary of the first performance of *Trial by Jury* in 1875. The evening consisted of a specially-written curtain-raiser, *Dramatic Licence* by William Douglas-Home, followed by performances of *Trial by Jury* and *The Sorcerer* and concluded with speeches by Prime Minister Harold Wilson and Bridget D'Oyly Carte. All the operas (except *Thespis*) were presented in sequence during the season, ending with a new production of *Utopia Limited* and a concert performance of *The Grand Duke*.

Shortly after the end of the Centenary Season, Bridget D'Oyly Carte was created a Dame Commander of the Order of the British Empire. Other honours awarded to members of the Company during these years were the O.B.E. awarded to Isidore Godfrey in June 1965, to Frederic Lloyd in January 1970 and to John Reed in June 1977.

There were a number of Royal occasions during this time. Prince Philip and Prince Andrew attended the Centenary Season performance of *The Gondoliers* on April 3, 1975, and Her Majesty The Queen attended the same opera in 1976 and *The Mikado* in 1968. The Duke of Gloucester attended a Gala Evening at the Savoy and the first night of the new *Iolanthe* production in 1977. Also in Jubilee Year the Company gave a Royal Command Performance of *H.M.S. Pinafore* at Windsor Castle on June 16, 1977, attended by most of the Royal Family. This was the first D'Oyly Carte performance at Windsor since that of *The Gondoliers* before Queen Victoria in 1891.

The Company continued to tour both nationally and internationally. In addition to North American tours in 1962–63, 1964–65, 1966–67, 1968 (Summer), 1968–69, 1976 (the 'Centenary tour') and 1978, the Company performed *The Mikado* and *H.M.S Pinafore* in Denmark in 1970 and *The Mikado* and *Iolanthe* at the Teatro Olimpico in Rome in 1974. In 1979 the Company made a highly successful 17-week tour of Australia and New Zealand. This was the first visit ever paid by the Company to Australasia, although many former members have performed there over the years.

After the Australasian tour, John Reed felt that he needed a change and he retired from the Company in October 1979 after 20 years in the principal rôles and 28 years with the Company. Since then he has continued to perform in Gilbert and Sullivan operas and he occasionally returned to make guest appearances with the Company.

ABOVE *I wonder how long I've been asleep!*
Goodness gracious! my bacon!
John James Box (Malcolm Williams) suddenly
awakes from his slumbers and remembers the
rasher of bacon he has left on the gridiron.

CENTRE **A strip of photographs of Anthony Raffell as
Sergeant Bouncer, a lodging-house keeper.**

LEFT **Michael Rayner as James John Cox, a
journeyman hatter. He was a member of the
Company from 1971 to 1979.**

OPPOSITE **On November 6, 1972 a party was held at the
Royal Court Theatre, Liverpool to celebrate the 21st
anniversary of John Reed's joining the Company. At
this party Business Manager Herbert Newby
presented him with a 1919 Brock poster of** *The
Sorcerer,* **autographed by all the members of the
Company.**

LEFT ABOVE **Jeffrey Skitch as the Learned Judge. He was a member of the Company from 1952 to 1965.**

LEFT BELOW *Comes the broken flower –*
Comes the cheated maid.
Jennifer Toye as Angelina, the Plaintiff.

CENTRE **Counsel for the Plaintiff (Thomas Lawlor) informs the Learned Judge (Alfred Oldridge) that to marry two wives at a time is 'burglaree'.**

ABOVE TOP *Oh Angelina! Come thou into Court!*
The Usher (George Cook) summons the Plaintiff.

ABOVE **Frederic Lloyd and John Reed at a recording session of *Trial by Jury* in June 1974.**

On March 29, 1971 at the Opera House, Manchester, *The Sorcerer* was revived for the first time since 1940 when the scenery and costumes were destroyed. In this new production the producer was Michael Heyland and the sets and costumes were designed by Osbert Lancaster, C.B.E. (see page 120).

ABOVE **John Wellington Wells (John Reed) prepares his love-philtre, watched by Aline and Alexis (Julia Goss and Ralph Mason).**

RIGHT **John Ayldon as Sir Marmaduke Pointdextre, an elderly baronet. He was a member of the Company from 1967 until its demise in 1982.**

OPPOSITE PAGE

ABOVE **Osbert Lancaster's attractive stage set, showing the exterior of Sir Marmaduke Pointdextre's Elizabethan mansion in the village of Ploverleigh.**

BELOW LEFT *I am welling over with limpid joy!* **Malcolm Williams as Alexis Pointdextre.**

BELOW RIGHT *I was a pale young curate then!* **Kenneth Sandford as Dr Daly, Vicar of Ploverleigh.**

ABOVE *A maiden fair to see,*
The pearl of minstrelsy,
A bud of blushing beauty
Jennifer Toye as Josephine, the Captain's daughter.
She was a member of the Company from 1953 to 1965,
and was the niece of Geoffrey Toye who conducted
the 1919–20, 1921–22 and 1924 London seasons,
rewrote the *Ruddigore* overture in 1921 and directed
the music for the 1938/9 film of *The Mikado*.

ABOVE LEFT *The maiden treats my suit with scorn,*
Rejects my humble gift, my lady;
She says I am ignobly born,
And cuts my hope adrift, my lady.
In this scene from the Finale of Act 1, Ralph
Rackstraw (Ralph Mason) tells Cousin Hebe (Pauline
Wales) of his rejection by Josephine. The set and
costumes for this production were by Peter Goffin.

BELOW LEFT Little Buttercup (Patricia Leonard) tries
to sell her wares to Bill Bobstay, Bob Becket and
Dick Deadeye (Gareth Jones, Michael Buchan and
John Ayldon). This photograph was taken during
the 1979 tour of Australia and New Zealand.

On June 16, 1977, in Silver Jubilee Year, the Company performed *H.M.S. Pinafore* at Windsor Castle
at an evening party given by Her Majesty The
Queen and His Royal Highness the Duke of
Edinburgh. This historic occasion was the Company's first performance at Windsor Castle since
The Gondoliers was presented before Queen Victoria in 1891 (see page 49).

ABOVE TOP The Waterloo Chamber at Windsor
Castle with the *H.M.S. Pinafore* set.

ABOVE Dame Bridget D'Oyly Carte and Frederic
Lloyd present Her Majesty The Queen with a set
of silver toast racks and tea strainers engraved
with the D'Oyly Carte crest and an inscription
commemorating the Command Performance.

OPPOSITE **The Pirate King** – one of a series of posters designed for the Company by Peter Goffin and featuring various characters from the operas.

LEFT *The sad, sad tale of the lonely orphan boy!* **Major-General Stanley (James Conroy-Ward)** and (above) the **Pirate King (Donald Adams)** weep with pity when the former claims to be an orphan.

ABOVE *Take any heart – take mine!* **Valerie Masterson as Mabel Stanley.**

INSET *Oh, false one, you have deceived me!* **Frederic (Philip Potter)** denounces **Ruth (Gillian Knight)**, the pirate maid-of-all-work, for deceiving him about her personal appearance.

187

Patience

ABOVE *I can't help it. I'm not a free agent.
I do it on compulsion.*
**Archibald Grosvenor (Kenneth Sandford) becomes a
commonplace young man at the end of the opera.**

ABOVE RIGHT *There is a strange magic in this love of ours!
Rivals as we all are in the affections of our Reginald, the
very hopelessness of our love is a bond that binds us to one
another.*
**Lady Angela (Beryl Dixon), Lady Saphir (Beti Lloyd-
Jones) and Lady Ella (Mary Sansom), three of the
rapturous maidens, brood on their infatuation for
the poet Bunthorne.**

CENTRE *Sing "Hey to you – good day to you" –
Sing "Bah to you – ha! ha! to you" –
Sing "Booh to you – pooh, pooh to you" –
And that's what I shall say!*
**Gillian Knight as Lady Jane and John Reed as
Reginald Bunthorne decide how to deal with
Archibald Grosvenor.**

BELOW RIGHT *But, as far as we can judge, it's something
like this sort of thing.*
Donald Adams as an aesthetic Colonel Calverley.

OPPOSITE *Toffee in moderation is a capital thing. But to
live on toffee – toffee for breakfast, toffee for dinner, toffee
for tea – to have it supposed that you care for nothing but
toffee, and that you would consider yourself insulted if
anything but toffee were offered to you – how would you like
that?*
Ralph Mason as the listless Duke of Dunstable.

FAR LEFT ABOVE *For we're to be married to-day – to-day!*
For we're to be married to-day!
Michael Rayner and Linda Anne Hutchison as
Strephon and Phyllis.

FAR LEFT BELOW *Taradiddle, taradiddle, tol lol lay!*
The Lord Chancellor (John Reed) enjoys a joke with
the Chorus of Peers.

LEFT ABOVE *Be your law the ancient saw,*
"Faint heart never won fair lady".
Lord Mountararat (John Ayldon) gives some
friendly advice to the Lord Chancellor (John Reed),
aided by Lord Tolloller (Geoffrey Shovelton).

LEFT **A new production of *Iolanthe* was presented at**
Sadler's Wells Theatre, London, on July 12, 1977. The
sets and costumes for this production were designed
by Bruno Santini, including this set for the
beginning of Act 1 depicting Fairyland. At the entry
of the Peers, the cobweb disappears, revealing an
Arcadian landscape.

ABOVE *Oh, amorous dove! Type of Ovidius Naso!*
Patricia Leonard as the Queen of the Fairies in the
dress designed by Bruno Santini (see also page 120).

OPPOSITE **John Reed as the disagreeable King Gama.**

TOP *Three hulking brothers more or less don't matter.*
James Conroy-Ward, Michael Rayner and Jon Ellison as Guron, Arac and Scynthius, King Gama's warrior sons.

ABOVE **Princess Ida (Barbara Lilley) converses with Melissa (Jane Metcalfe) and Lady Psyche (Julia Goss), watched by her lady undergraduates.**

RIGHT **King Hildebrand (Kenneth Sandford) reminds Princess Ida (Barbara Lilley) of her oath to Hilarion.**

LEFT *My little bride that was to have been!*
Nanki-Poo (Geoffrey Shovelton) embraces Yum-Yum (Julia Goss) to the distress of Ko-Ko (John Reed) who has just ascertained that if Nanki-Poo is beheaded then Yum-Yum will be buried alive.

BELOW *But youth, of course, must have its fling.*
The three little maids from school (Peggy Ann Jones, Gillian Humphreys and Jennifer Toye) enjoy themselves at the expense of Pooh-Bah (Kenneth Sandford).

BOTTOM *Bow – Bow – to his daughter-in-law elect!*
Patricia Leonard as Katisha, an elderly lady in love with Nanki-Poo. She was a member of the Company from 1972 until its demise in 1982, assuming the soubrette rôles before moving on to the contralto rôles in 1977.

CENTRE *Beware! Beware! Beware!*
Donald Adams as Sir Roderic Murgatroyd, the 21st Baronet of Ruddigore.

LEFT ABOVE **Another characterization of Sir Roderic Murgatroyd, as portrayed by John Ayldon.**

LEFT BELOW *Now tell me pray, and tell me true,*
What in the world should the young man do?
Robin Oakapple (John Reed) timidly seeks the advice of pretty Rose Maybud (Mary Sansom).

ABOVE TOP *Though she lived alone, apart,*
Hope lay nestling at her heart.
Peggy Ann Jones as Mad Margaret in Act 1, madly in love with Sir Despard Murgatroyd.

ABOVE **Leonard Osborn, the Dick Dauntless of the 1950s, teaches Meston Reid the finer points of the hornpipe.**

LEFT **John Reed as Jack Point, a strolling jester, and Thomas Lawlor as Sir Richard Cholmondeley, the Lieutenant of the Tower.**

ABOVE TOP *When maiden loves she sits and sighs,
She wanders to and fro.*
As the curtain rises on Act 1, Phoebe Meryll (Jane Metcalfe) is discovered at her spinning wheel.

ABOVE *This is our joy-day unalloyed!*
Colonel Fairfax and Elsie Maynard (Thomas Round and Ann Hood) embrace at the end of the opera.

A controversial new production of *The Gondoliers* was presented at the Saville Theatre, London, on January 29, 1968. The producer was Anthony Besch with stage sets by John Stoddart and costumes by Luciana Arrighi.

ABOVE *Oh, bury, bury – let the grave close o'er*
The days that were – that never will be more!
Colin Wright and Julia Goss as Luiz and Casilda.

ABOVE RIGHT *I said to myself, "That man is a Duke, and I will love him." Several of my relations bet me I couldn't, but I did – desperately!*
John Reed and Lyndsie Holland as the Duke and Duchess of Plaza-Toro at the Court of Barataria.

ABOVE FAR RIGHT **Luciana Arrighi with some of her costume designs.**

RIGHT *We are Venetian gondoliers – your equals in everything except our calling, and in that at once your masters and your servants.*
Thomas Lawlor as Giuseppe Palmieri with Ralph Mason as Marco and Kenneth Sandford as Don Alhambra del Bolero, Grand Inquisitor of Spain.

FAR RIGHT **Frederic Lloyd presents Michael Rayner, Julia Goss, Kenneth Sandford and Lyndsie Holland to Her Majesty the Queen at a performance of** *The Gondoliers* **on February 25, 1976.**

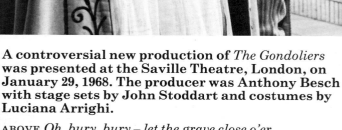

200

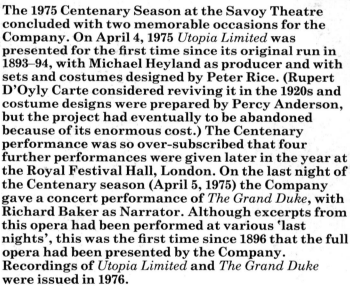

The 1975 Centenary Season at the Savoy Theatre concluded with two memorable occasions for the Company. On April 4, 1975 *Utopia Limited* was presented for the first time since its original run in 1893–94, with Michael Heyland as producer and with sets and costumes designed by Peter Rice. (Rupert D'Oyly Carte considered reviving it in the 1920s and costume designs were prepared by Percy Anderson, but the project had eventually to be abandoned because of its enormous cost.) The Centenary performance was so over-subscribed that four further performances were given later in the year at the Royal Festival Hall, London. On the last night of the Centenary season (April 5, 1975) the Company gave a concert performance of *The Grand Duke*, with Richard Baker as Narrator. Although excerpts from this opera had been performed at various 'last nights', this was the first time since 1896 that the full opera had been presented by the Company. Recordings of *Utopia Limited* and *The Grand Duke* were issued in 1976.

FAR LEFT ABOVE *With wily brain upon the spot*
A private plot we'll plan.
John Reed and John Ayldon as Scaphio and Phantis, Judges of the Utopian Supreme Court, hatch a plan to foil King Paramount.

FAR LEFT Kenneth Sandford as King Paramount.

ABOVE LEFT Meston Reid as Captain Fitzbattleaxe of the First Life Guards. He was a member of the Company from 1974 until its demise in 1982.

LEFT Lyndsie Holland as Lady Sophy, an English Gouvernante. She was a member of the Company from 1971 to 1977 and played the leading contralto rôles.

ABOVE The record sleeve for the Company's recording of *The Grand Duke*.

TOP LEFT **John Ayldon, Julia Goss, Michael Rayner and Pamela Field prepare to visit Rome in 1974.**

BELOW LEFT **Sir Malcolm Sargent and James Walker at a recording of** *The Yeomen of the Guard* **in 1964.**

TOP RIGHT **A celebration party in Leeds for the centenary of** *The Sorcerer* **on November 17, 1977.**

LEFT **Bridget D'Oyly Carte gives a party to celebrate the award of the O.B.E. to Isidore Godfrey.**

ABOVE **Bridget D'Oyly Carte officially opens the** *Gilbert & Sullivan*, **a Whitbread pub in London.**

The Curtain Falls

James Conroy-Ward as John Wellington Wells in *The Sorcerer*

James Conroy-Ward joined the Company from Covent Garden in July 1973 as a member of the Chorus and understudy to John Reed. He took over the comedy rôles in 1979 after the tour of Australia and New Zealand. The company at this time was in good heart with Kenneth Sandford as the doyen of the team, well supported by a strong cast including John Ayldon, Patricia Leonard, Barbara Lilley and Meston Reid. Royston Nash, successor as Musical Director to Isidore Godfrey and James Walker, had left in early 1979 and his place at the podium was taken by Fraser Goulding.

At this time, both management and singers had been led to believe by the Arts Council that the D'Oyly Carte Company was to become the National Light Opera Company of Great Britain, performing both Gilbert and Sullivan operas and works by other composers, such as *Merrie England*. In fact, the first work to be suggested was *Véronique* by André Messager and the costs of such a production were calculated. The Arts Council asked the Company to cancel planned touring dates in the Autumn of 1979 for a special period of rehearsals and it was clearly understood by the Company that financial support would be forthcoming.

Unfortunately, while the Company was touring in Australia, the Arts Council suddenly informed the management that it could not proceed with the idea as it had no money available. An autumn tour was hurriedly arranged, but all the best dates had gone and, as a result of playing in smaller theatres, a considerable loss was incurred. During 1980 many cities and towns throughout Britain were visited, but it was becoming clear to the D'Oyly Carte Trustees that without a very considerable grant from the Arts Council, preferably for a period of at least three years, it would not be possible for the Company to continue. It had once been feasible for touring com-

panies to make a profit, as did the D'Oyly Carte in its earlier days, but with ever-increasing costs of production and travelling, this was no longer the case. Because of this, the Company was fortunate in having sponsors – Barclay's Bank, the Hanson Trust, the Ellerman Trust and others – who gave considerable help in the final years.

Meanwhile, an enquiry was set up by the Arts Council's Music Panel and Touring Committee to investigate the demand for light opera in Britain and to suggest ways in which such a demand might be met. Particular attention was to be paid to the problems of touring companies, with the D'Oyly Carte Company singled out for special consideration.

The Committee met several times in 1979–80 and recommended in its report that the Arts Council should 'receive sympathetically an application from the D'Oyly Carte Company for financial assistance', suggesting a sum of £50,000–£100,000 per year over, say, three years. The report concluded: 'The greatest fear, however, and in our view overriding all others is that D'Oyly Carte could disappear, and the loss would be felt in almost every major provincial city in the country as well as in London.'

The Arts Council, itself facing severe financial problems, rejected its Committee's recommendations and gave no money to the Company. A 'Save the D'Oyly Carte' appeal was started, but it failed to raise sufficient money in time.

The farewell season took place at the Adelphi Theatre, London, from November 18, 1981 to February 27, 1982, with John Reed and Valerie Masterson as guest artists and Sir Charles Mackerras and Alexander Faris as guest conductors. On the last night, after a speech from the stage by Frederic Lloyd and a few words of farewell from the Royal Box by Dame Bridget D'Oyly Carte, the curtain fell for the last time.

One hundred and seven years is an impressive lifespan for an opera company. During this time the D'Oyly Carte Company was a 'source of innocent merriment' for countless millions of people. D'Oyly Carte has become, and will always remain, an important chapter in the history of the theatre.

ABOVE *Retire, my daughter, to your cabin – take this, his photograph, with you – it may help to bring you to a more reasonable frame of mind.*
Captain Corcoran (Clive Harré) tries to persuade his daughter Josephine (Vivian Tierney) to accept Sir Joseph Porter's hand in marriage.

LEFT *Over the bright blue sea*
  Comes Sir Joseph Porter, K.C.B.,
    Wherever he may go
  Bang-bang the loud nine-pounders go!
    Shout o'er the bright blue sea
  For Sir Joseph Porter, K.C.B.
James Conroy-Ward as the Ruler of the Queen's Navee.

OPPOSITE PAGE

ABOVE *The policeman's lot is a happy one!*
An energetic *Tarantara* from the Chorus of Policemen on the sea-shore at Blackpool.

BELOW *We've got a little list!*
James Conroy-Ward meets Grahame Clifford, who played the comedy rôles throughout the war, during the Company's 1979 tour of Australasia.

OPPOSITE PAGE *Iolanthe*

ABOVE *Thou the tree and I the flower –*
Thou the idol; I the throng –
Thou the day and I the hour –
Thou the singer; I the song!
The husband-and-wife team of Peter Lyon (Strephon) and Barbara Lilley (Phyllis).

BELOW LEFT *And in my court I sit all day,*
Giving agreeable girls away.
With one for him – and one for he –
James Conroy-Ward as the Lord Chancellor.

BELOW RIGHT *Every heart and every hand*
In our loving little band
Welcomes thee to Fairyland,
Iolanthe!
Lorraine Daniels in the title rôle.

THIS PAGE *The Pirates of Penzance*

ABOVE **The Centenary Performance of** *The Pirates of Penzance* **was given at Sadler's Wells Theatre, London, on December 31, 1979. Pictured around the anniversary cake are John Ayldon (Pirate King) and Meston Reid (Frederic) with Fraser Goulding and Sir Charles Mackerras (conductors) and Frederic Lloyd (General Manager). Sir Charles Mackerras is well known for his arrangement of Sullivan's music for the ballet** *Pineapple Poll*, **and he has conducted a number of D'Oyly Carte performances.**

LEFT **Vivian Tierney as Mabel with Alistair Donkin as Major-General Stanley.**

AN EVENING OF EXCERPTS from the D'Oyly Carte repertoire: Cox & Box 1866 ◇ Thespis 1871 ◇ Trial by Jury 1875 ◇ The Sorcerer 1877 ◇ HMS Pinafore 1878 ◇ The Pirates of Penzance 1880 ◇ Patience 1881 ◇ Iolanthe 1882 ◇ Princess Ida 1884 ◇ The Mikado 1885 ◇ Ruddigore 1887 ◇ The Yeomen of the Guard 1888 ◇ The Gondoliers 1889 ◇ Utopia Limited 1893 ◇ The Grand Duke 1896 ◇ ◇ ◇ and including a Concert Overture based on Savoy Opera themes composed by Paul Seeley

PRINCIPAL ARTISTES ~ Kenneth Sandford ◇ John Ayldon ◇ James Conroy-Ward ◇ Lorraine Daniels ◇ Clive Harré ◇ Patricia Leonard ◇ Peter Lyon ◇ Meston Reid ◇ Geoffrey Shovelton ◇ Vivian Tierney ◇ ◇ ◇ GENTLEMEN OF THE CHORUS ~ Clive Birch ◇ Neil Braithwaite ◇ Michael Buchan ◇ Barry Clark ◇ Philip Creasy ◇ Alistair Donkin ◇ Robert Gibbs ◇ Bruce Graham ◇ Michael Hamlett ◇ Peter James-Robinson ◇ Michael Lessiter ◇ Thomas Marandola ◇ Guy Matthews ◇ Sean Osborne ◇ Alan Rice ◇ Thomas Scholey ◇ ◇ ◇ LADIES OF THE CHORUS ~ Pamela Baxter ◇ Susan Cochrane ◇ Linda Darnell ◇ Riona Faram ◇ Christine George ◇ Alexandra Hann ◇ Suzanne Houlden ◇ Beti Lloyd-Jones ◇ Margaret Lynn-Williams ◇ Roberta Morrell ◇ Jill Pert ◇ Jane Stanford ◇ Ann-Louise Straker ◇ Caroline Tatlow ◇ Hélène Witcombe ◇ ◇ ◇

D'OYLY CARTE
IN ASSOCIATION WITH BARCLAYS BANK · PRESENTS

GILBERT & SULLIVAN

ADELPHI THEATRE
STRAND WC2
NOVEMBER 18 – FEBRUARY 27

The world's best-loved musicals

GLC assisted

The final season of the D'Oyly Carte Opera Company took place at the Adelphi Theatre, London, from November 18, 1981 to February 27, 1982. In addition to the regular Company there were guest appearances by John Reed, Valerie Masterson, Alexander Faris and Sir Charles Mackerras. A lively new production of *The Mikado* was well received by the London critics.

OPPOSITE PAGE At the start of the Adelphi Theatre season, the Company gave four carol concerts in the Covent Garden piazza. These concerts raised a substantial amount for cancer research. Pictured here are Patricia Leonard (above) and John Ayldon, James Conroy-Ward and Geoffrey Shovelton (below).

LEFT An advertising poster for the final season.

ABOVE The final Last Night was a memorable occasion, full of the usual jollity but necessarily tinged with sadness. As can be seen from the programme (designed by Geoffrey Shovelton), the evening consisted of excerpts from the repertoire, beginning with *Cox and Box* and *Thespis* and ending with *The Grand Duke*. The final chorus of the evening was *We leave you with feelings of pleasure* from *The Gondoliers*.

213

Bibliography

There are hundreds of books relating to Gilbert and Sullivan and their operas. The following list is intended to provide a representative selection.

ALLEN, Reginald, *The First Night Gilbert and Sullivan*, The Limited Editions Club and The Heritage Club, New York, 1958, and Chappell, London, 1975.
AYRE, Leslie, *The Gilbert and Sullivan Companion*, W. H. Allen, London and New York, 1972.
BAILY, Leslie, *The Gilbert and Sullivan Book*, Cassell, London, 1952.
BAILY, Leslie, *Gilbert and Sullivan and Their World,* Thames and Hudson, London, 1973.
BRADLEY, Ian, *The Annotated Gilbert and Sullivan,* Penguin Books, London, 1982.
CELLIER, François, and BRIDGEMAN, Cunningham, *Gilbert, Sullivan and D'Oyly Carte*, London, 1914.
D'OYLY CARTE OPERA TRUST, *100 Years of D'Oyly Carte and Gilbert and Sullivan* (Centenary Booklet), London, 1975.
GILBERT, W. S., *The Savoy Operas*, MacMillan, London, 1956.
JACOBS, Arthur, *Arthur Sullivan – A Victorian Musician*, Oxford University Press, Oxford, 1984.
JEFFERSON, Alan, *The Complete Gilbert & Sullivan Opera Guide*, Webb & Bower, Exeter, 1984.
MANDER, Raymond, and MITCHENSON, Joe, *A Picture History of Gilbert and Sullivan*, Vista Books, London and New York, 1962.
PEARSON, Hesketh, *Gilbert, His Life and Strife*, Methuen, London, 1957.
ROLLINS, Cyril, and WITTS, R. John, *The D'Oyly Carte Opera Company in Gilbert and Sullivan Operas*, Michael Joseph, London, 1962.
SMITH, Geoffrey, *The Savoy Operas*, Hale, London, 1983.
WOOD, Roger, *A D'Oyly Carte Album*, Adam and Charles Black, London, 1953.

Index of Operas and Plays

Ages Ago 14
Beauty Stone, The 50, 74
Chieftain, The 59
Contrabandista, The 14
Cox and Box 65, 91, 129, 155, 179
Emerald Isle, The 80
GONDOLIERS, THE 2, 47, 83, 112, 115, 121, 122, 148, 168, 200
Grand Duchess of Gerolstein, The 74
GRAND DUKE, THE 60, 203
Haddon Hall 55
H.M.S. PINAFORE 20, 43, 65, 66, 77, 96, 132, 158, 176, 184, 209
IOLANTHE 4, 30, 71, 85, 102, 138, 162, 190, 210
Ivanhoe 53
Lucky Star, The 74
Merrie England 81
MIKADO, THE 36, 43, 64, 70, 86, 106, 113, 115, 151, 164, 194
Nautch Girl, The 55
PATIENCE 5, 26, 29, 67, 71, 72, 79, 84, 100, 136, 152, 160, 188
Périchole, La 16
PIRATES OF PENZANCE, THE 22, 78, 86, 98, 114, 134, 159, 186, 211
PRINCESS IDA 3, 32, 104, 126, 140, 170, 192
Rose of Persia, The 74
RUDDIGORE 40, 70, 108, 114, 144, 151, 166, 196
SORCERER, THE 18, 35, 76, 94, 131, 155, 182, 206
THESPIS 15
TRIAL BY JURY 16, 35, 76, 92, 130, 151, 156, 173, 180
UTOPIA LIMITED 56, 113, 202
Vicar of Bray, The 54
YEOMEN OF THE GUARD, THE 1, 10, 44, 70, 73, 82, 110, 115, 146, 167, 198

Index of Names

Abbott, Margery 139
Adams, Donald 6, 154, 158, 161, 165, 187–8, 197
Andean, Richard 84
Arrighi, Luciana 201
Ayldon, John 182, 184, 190, 196, 202, 204, 211–2

Baker, Kenny 142
Barnett, Alice 22, 26, 30
Barrett, Alan 168
Barrington, Jean 166
Barrington, Rutland 19, 23, 31, 33, 35, 37, 41, 47, 54–5, 57, 87
Baxter, Maisie 101
Billington, Fred 76
Blain, Clarice 174
Bond, Jessie 30, 39, 42, 46
Braham, Leonora 27, 33, 39, 42
Brandram, Rosina 33, 43, 57–8, 73, 78, 81
Briercliffe, Nellie 95–6, 98, 105
Brownlow, Wallace 49
Buchan, Michael 184

Cammidge, George 129
Cecil, Sylvia 93, 105, 112
Cellier, François 57
Clifford, Grahame 142, 147, 149, 208
Colin, Jean 142
Colman, Ronald 90
Conroy-Ward, James 187, 193, 206–210, 212
Cook, George 155, 181
Coomber, Lilian 82
Crompton, Reginald 80

Daniels, Lorraine 210
Darnton, Leo 91, 93, 104
Dean, John 128–9, 131, 136–7, 147–8
Denny, Doreen 101
Denny, W. H. 46, 48, 55–7
Dickson, Muriel 97, 100, 135, 146, 148
Dixon, Beryl 172, 188
Dolaro, Selina 16
Donkin, Alistair 211
Dow, Clara 84–5
D'Oyly Carte, Bridget 6, 8–9, 185, 205
D'Oyly Carte, Helen 9, 57
D'Oyly Carte, Richard 9, 13, 52, 57
D'Oyly Carte, Rupert 9, 123
Drummond-Grant, Ann 131, 140, 146, 161–2, 169
Dudley, John 149
Duke of Edinburgh 8

Elburn, Beatrice 90
Ellison, Jon 193
Evans, Eleanor 90
Evans, Ivor 156
Evans, Maurice 173
Evett, Robert 74, 77, 79–80
Eyre, Marjorie 90, 97, 101, 107, 128, 136, 138, 147–8

Fancourt, Darrell 90–1, 103, 106, 128, 132, 134, 136
Farren, Nellie 15
Federici, F. 37
Ferguson, Catherine 98, 103, 109
Field, Pamela 204
Finch, Peter 173
Flynn, Radley 144
Fryatt, John 172

Gardiner, Evelyn 133, 149
Garry, Herbert 138, 148
Gelsthorpe, Blossom 90
German, Edward 80
Gilbert, Lady 123
Gilbert, W. S. 57
Gill, Dorothy 136
Gilliland, Helen 102, 110
Gillingham, Joan 151

Godfrey, Isidore 123, 205
Goffin, Peter 144
Gordon, J. M. 105
Goss, Julia 182, 193–4, 200–1, 204
Goulding, Charles 95, 140
Goulding, Fraser 211
Granville, Sydney 91, 98, 102, 104, 128, 130, 135
Gray, Warwick 34
Green, Martyn 124–6, 128–9, 131, 133–8, 142–4, 146, 149
Green, Richard 53, 55, 83
Grey, Sibyl 39
Gridley, Lawrence 57
Griffin, Elsie 94, 98, 109
Griffin, Joseph 99
Griffiths, Neville 159
Grossmith, George 10–12, 19–20, 27, 30, 32, 35–6, 41, 70

Habbick, Jack 157
Halman, Ella 137, 145
Harding, Muriel 159–60, 167
Harré, Clive 209
Harris, Charles 57
Haste, Harry 174
Hay, James 98, 105
Herlie, Eileen 173
Hewson, Jones 62, 73, 78–80
Hindmarsh, Jean 168, 170
Hobbs, Frederick 111
Holland, Lyndsie 200–2
Hood, Ann 199
Hood, Marion 23
Humphreys, Gillian 195
Hutchison, Linda Anne 190
Hynd, Alice 157

Jay, Isabel 76, 78–80
Jones, Gareth 184
Jones, Peggy Ann 195, 197
Joran, Pauline 74

Kenningham, Charles 53, 57–8, 64
King George V 121
Knight, Gillian 187–8

Lawlor, Thomas 181, 199–200
Lawson, Winifred 95, 100, 107
Lely, Durward 27, 31, 33, 36, 41
Leon, W. H. 79
Leonard, Patricia 184, 191, 195, 212
Lewis, Bertha 90, 95, 97, 100–1, 103, 105–8, 111–12, 122
Lilley, Barbara 193, 210
Lloyd, Frederic 8, 181, 185, 201, 211
Lloyd George, David 124–5
Lloyd-Jones, Beti 188
Lugg, William 34
Lyon, Peter 210
Lytton, Henry 74, 76, 77, 79–81, 86, 88–90, 94–6, 100–1, 103, 105–7, 109–10, 112, 122–5

Mackerras, Sir Charles 211
Marsh, Yvonne 173
Marsland, James 157
Mason, Ralph 182, 184, 189, 201
Masterson, Valerie 187
McIntosh, Nancy 57–8
Metcalfe, Jane 193, 199
Milne, Ella 98
Mitchell, Margaret 151
Moody, Eileen 148
Moore, Decima 49
Morey, Cynthia 172
Morgan, Fisher 154, 157, 163, 170
Morley, Robert 173
Moss, Strafford 86

Naylor, Kathleen 136, 139
Newby, Herbert 178
Nickell-Lean, Elizabeth 107

Oldham, Derek 94, 96, 104, 109–10
Oldridge, Alfred 180

Osborn, Leonard 144, 161–2, 167, 170, 197
Owen, Emmie 57–8, 62, 77

Palmay, Ilka von 63
Passmore, Walter 50–1, 57, 59, 61, 64, 74, 76, 77–9, 81
Paul, Mrs Howard 19
Penley, W. S. 17
Perry, Florence 57–8
Pointer, Sidney 103
Potter, Philip 187
Pounds, Courtice 44, 47–8
Pounds, Louie 80
Power, George 20
Pratt, Peter 152–4, 158–60, 162, 164, 166–8

Queen Elizabeth II 185, 201
Queen Mary 121
Queen Victoria 49

Raffell, Anthony 179
Rands, Leslie 90–2, 103, 128, 130, 132, 149
Rayner, Michael 179, 190, 193, 201, 204
Reed, John 6, 8, 155–6, 161, 176–8, 181–2, 188, 190–2, 194, 196, 198, 201–2
Reid, Meston 197, 203, 211
René, Louie 83–4
Richards, Arthur 164
Ripple, Pacie 82–3
Ronald, Rowena 103
Rose, Jessie 82
Round, Thomas 159, 164, 168, 173, 199
Rowe, Louise 54

St. John, Florence 74
Sanders, Ivy 139
Sanderson, May 157
Sandford, Kenneth 6, 166–8, 183, 188, 193, 195, 201–2
Sansom, Mary 188, 196
Sargent, Sir Malcolm 204
Scott Fishe, R. 57, 59, 62, 64
Seymour, W. H. 57
Sheffield, Leo 93, 95–6, 99, 106, 110, 112
Shovelton, Geoffrey 191, 194, 212
Sinden, Frederick 155
Skitch, Jeffrey 180
Sladen, Victoria 171
Styler, Alan 155, 167–8
Sullivan, Sir Arthur 57
Sullivan, Frederic 15–16
Sumner, William 136

Temple, Richard 19–20, 23, 27, 34, 37
Thornton, Eric 155, 158
Thornton, Frank 26–7
Tierney, Vivian 209, 211
Toole, J. L. 15
Toye, Jennifer 169, 180, 185, 195
Tunks, Leicester 86

Ulmar, Geraldine 42–3

Vincent, Ruth 73, 77

Wales, Pauline 184
Walker, James 204
Walker, Richard 128, 130, 133
Watson, Richard 141, 144
Wilde, Harold 84
Williams, Malcolm 179, 183
Wilson, Frank 84
Wilson, Lord, of Rievaulx 7
Wilson, Robert 92
Wilson, Robin 8
Wood, Frank 15
Workman, C. H. 62, 82, 86–7
Worsley, Bruce 175
Wright, Colin 200
Wright, Joyce 151, 154, 158, 163, 167–8
Wyatt, Frank 47

Yaw, Ellen Beach 75

Acknowledgements

Abbreviations: L = left, C = centre, R = right; T = top, I = inset
B = bottom.

Photographs and illustrations are supplied by, or reproduced by kind permission of the following: Alpert Le Vine 193BR; John Blomfield 9BR, 169TR, 179L, 180BL, 180–181C, 184T, 186TL, 186TR, 187I, 189, 194–195C, 198–199C, 200–201BC, 205BL; British Film Institute 173BR; The British Library 39B; The Daily Express 107BR, 124I; The Daily Herald 125TR; The Daily News Chronicle 125BR; The Daily Sketch 39B; The Daily Telegraph 125CR; The D'Oyly Carte Archive 1, 2L, 2–3C, 4, 5, 9TL, 9TR, 9BL, 10–11, 13T, 13B, 14T, 14B, 15T, 15B, 16, 16I, 17T, 17B, 18T, 18B, 19TL, 19TR, 19B, 20BL, 20BC, 20BR, 21T, 21B, 22TL, 22BL, 22–23C, 23TL, 23TR, 23B, 24T, 24B, 25, 26TL, 26TR, 26B, 27TL, 27TR, 29T, 29B, 30TL, 30BL, 30–31C, 31TR, 32, 33T, 33BL, 33BC, 33BR, 34T, 34BL, 34BR, 35TL, 35TR, 35B, 36, 36I, 37TL, 37TR, 37B, 38T, 38B, 39TL, 40–41, 41TL, 41TR, 41BL, 41BR, 42T, 42BR, 43TL, 43TR, 43B, 44TL, 44TR, 44BL, 45, 46T, 46B, 47T, 47B, 48–49TC, 48B, 49T, 49C, 49BL, 50–51, 52, 53TL, 53TR, 53B, 54, 54I, 55TL, 55TR, 55B, 56, 57B, 58T, 58BL, 59T, 59BL, 59BR, 60B, 61, 62TL, 62BC, 62–63C, 63R, 64TL, 64TR, 64B, 65TR, 68–9, 73TL, 73TR, 73BR, 74TL, 74TC, 74TR, 74BL, 75, 76TL, 77TL, 77TR, 77B, 78TL, 78TR, 78BL, 78BR, 79TL, 79TR, 79B, 80T, 80BR, 81T, 81BL, 81BR, 82T, 82B, 83T, 83B, 84T, 84I, 84B, 85, 86–87T, 86B, 87T, 87B, 88–89, 90, 91TL, 91TR (Stage Photo Co.), 91B, 92–93T, 92B, 93TR, 93B, 94, 95TL (Stage Photo Co.), 95TR, 95B, 96TL, 96BL, 96–97C, 97TR, 97BR (Stage Photo Co.), 98TL, 98BL, 98–99C, 99TR, 100TL, 100TR, 100BL, 100–101BC, 101TL (Stage Photo Co.), 101TR (Stage Photo Co.), 102, 103TL (Stage Photo Co.), 103BL, 103TR (Campbell's Press Studio), 103BR (Stage Photo Co.), 104B, 105TR (Stage Photo Co.), 105B (Stage Photo Co.), 106TL, 106BL, 106–107C, 107TR (Stage Photo Co.), 108T (Stage Photo Co.), 108B (Stage Photo Co.), 109TL, 109TR, 109B, 110TL, 110TR, 110–111BC, 111TR, 111BR, 112T, 112B (Stage Photo Co.), 121, 122–123T (Underwood Commercial Studios Ltd.), 122BL (Stage Photo Co.), 122BR, 123TR, 123BL, 126–127, 128 (Cosmo-Sileo Co.), 129T, 129B, 130 (Stage Photo Co.), 130I, 131L (Bassano Ltd.), 132, 133TL (Lucas and Pritchard Studio),

133TR (Lucas and Pritchard Studio), 133BL (De Bellis Studio), 134L, 134–135C, 135R (Stage Photo Co.), 136T, 136BL, 136BR, 137TL (Campbell's Press Studio), 137TR, 137BR, 138TL, 138BL, 138–139C, 139R, 140, 140I (Stage Photo Co.), 141T, 141B, 142BL, 142TR, 144T, 144BL, 144BR, 145T, 145B, 146L (Stage Photo Co.), 146–147T, 146BR (Campbell's Press Studio), 147TR, 147CR, 147BL, 148L, 148TR (De Bellis Studio), 148BR, 149TL (Campbell's Press Studio), 149TR (Campbell's Press Studio), 149BL, 151TL (Decca), 168TL, 168CL, 168BL, 168–169C, 170TL (Houston Rogers), 170BL (Houston Rogers), 170–171C (Fred Sinden), 171R, 172TL, 172TR, 172B (Houston Rogers), 175T, 175B, 176–177, 179TR (Bob Johnson), 180TL (Donald Southern), 181TR, 182T, 182B, 183T (Donald Southern), 183BL, 183BR, 184B, 185TL (Guttenberg Ltd.), 186, 188TL, 188TR (Fred Sinden), 188CR (Fred Sinden), 188BR (Donald Southern), 190TL (John Silverside), 191TR, 195TR (Donald Southern), 195BR, 196TL, 196BL (Fred Sinden), 196–197C, 197TR (John Silverside), 198L (Donald Southern), 199BR (Donald Southern), 200TL (Donald Southern), 200–201TC, 202T, 202BL (Crispian Woodgate), 202–203BC (Crispian Woodgate), 203TR (Decca), 204T (J. A. Hamilton Studios Ltd.), 204B, 208B, 210T, 210BL, 210BR, 211T, 212T (J. A. Hamilton Studios Ltd.), 212B (J. A. Hamilton Studios Ltd.), 213T, 213B; Fox Photos 150–151; Keystone Press Agency 201TR; The Liverpool Weekly News 178; London Express News Service 7, 8T, 216T; London Film Productions 173T, 173BL, 173BR; The Manchester Daily Mail 208T; The Manchester Evening News 6L; Raymond Mander and Joe Mitchenson Theatre Collection 58BR, 60T, 76B; Mansell Collection 57T; National Portrait Gallery 12, 80BL; Notley Public Relations Services 205BR; The Pierpont Morgan Library endpapers, 39TR, 65T, 72T; The Press Association Ltd. 8B, 201BR; Punch 3B; Malcolm Rouse 190–191TC, 199TR; The Sphere 131R; Sport & General Press Agency Ltd. 123BR; Barry Swaebe 185TR, 185BR; Theatre Magazine (Institute) 42BL; Victoria and Albert Museum 27B, 28, 65B, 66, 67, 70BL, 70BR, 71T, 71BL, 72B, 113T, 113B, 114T, 114B, 115T, 115BL, 115BR, 116, 117TL, 117TR, 117B, 118L, 118TR, 118BR, 119TL, 119TC, 119TR, 119BL, 120TL, 120TR, 120BL, 120BR; John Watt Associates 179BL, 181BR, 197BR, 203TL; The Western Daily Press and Bristol Mirror 124; Reg Wilson 6R, 187TR, 190BL, 190–191BC, 192, 193T, 206–207, 209T, 209B, 211B; Roger Wood/Pictorial Press 142TL, 142–143, 151TR, 174TL, 174TR, 174BL, 174BR; The Yorkshire Post 205T.

Finished! At last! Finished!